Recreate the World
You Once Dreamed Of

"When I was a little girl, I thought that one day I would grow into perfection. This perfection held for all of us complete wisdom, happiness, and unconditional love. As I grew, somehow I learned to become fearful of the world. I lost all self-confidence and self-love. I was crushed when I lost hope of finding my perfect world."

Have you felt like this little girl? Are you now an adult who is disappointed in the way the world has turned out? Do you feel the empty void of a daily grind that seldom results in any real joy or meaning? Do you find people more difficult than easy to get along with? You are not alone.

Elizabeth Jean Rogers has written *Create Your Own Joy* as an answer to these destructive and altogether too common feelings. This beautifully written manual will gently guide you through the process of taking back the joy, wisdom, and power that has always been yours. *Create Your Own Joy* will become your own expression of yourself, a very personal and practical process of redefining your life in the terms you want to see and be. Rogers has devised a variety of stimulating and enriching exercises, such as guided meditations and journaling, so that your journey back to a world in which you feel at peace is interesting and integral. Absorbing chapters like "Turn Fear Into Confidence" and "Resolve All Challenges" give you the encouragement and direction to access your creative energy and inspiration so you can begin to live a fulfilling life now. You have the ability to create a joy-filled life—*Create Your Own Joy* will show you how.

Create Your Own Joy is a book written for you. It will be the book that rewards your time and energy with abundant returns for the rest of your life.

About the Author

Elizabeth Jean Rogers was born in a small town in Kentucky. The youngest of seven children in a caring, close-knit family, she was raised with strong traditional values. As a result of her upbringing she developed a code of ethics of caring and sincerity.

Ms. Rogers enjoys traveling, camping, and four-wheeling. She also has a love of art and her home is filled with her own paintings and sketches. She has read many books on the power of the mind, and has taken courses in Shiatsu, T'ai Chi, and Yoga. In 1989 Ms. Rogers attained first-degree certification in the Reiki principles and methods of natural healing. Currently she is compiling quotes and poems to comfort individuals who have lost a loved one, as did she.

The author hopes this book opens up new ideas and discoveries for you, the reader. These ideas have changed her life, given her power, and, indeed, have brought this book to you!

To Write to the Author

If you wish to contact the author or would like more information about this book, please write to the author in care of Llewellyn Worldwide and we will forward your request. Both the author and publisher appreciate hearing from you and learning of your enjoyment of this book and how it has helped you. Llewellyn Worldwide cannot guarantee that every letter written to the author can be answered, but all will be forwarded. Please write to:

Elizabeth Jean Rogers
c/o Llewellyn Worldwide
P.O. Box 64383-K354, St. Paul, MN 55164–0383, U.S.A.

Please enclose a self-addressed, stamped envelope for reply, or $1.00 to cover costs.
If outside the U.S.A., enclose international postal reply coupon.

Free Catalog From Llewellyn Worldwide

For more than 90 years Llewellyn has brought its readers knowledge in the fields of metaphysics and human potential. Learn about the newest books in spiritual guidance, natural healing, astrology, occult philosophy, and more. Enjoy book reviews, new age articles, a calendar of events, plus current advertised products and services. To get your free copy of *Llewellyn's New Worlds of Mind and Spirit,* send your name and address to:

Llewellyn's New Worlds of Mind and Spirit
P.O. Box 64383-K354, St. Paul, MN 55164-0383, U.S.A.

Create Your Own Joy

A Guide for Transforming Your Life

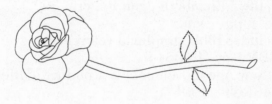

Elizabeth Jean Rogers

1994
Llewellyn Publications
St. Paul, Minnesota 55164-0383 U.S.A.

FIRST EDITION
First Printing, 1994

Cover design: Linda Norton
Interior art: Elizabeth Jean Rogers
Book design and layout: Jessica Thoreson and Elizabeth Jean Rogers
Editor: Jessica Thoreson

Library of Congress Cataloging-in-Publication Data
Rogers, Elizabeth J. (Elizabeth Jean), 1954–
    Create your own joy: a guide for transforming your
      life / Elizabeth Jean Rogers.
         p.   cm.
    Includes bibliographical references.
    ISBN 1-56718-354-9
    1. New Age movement. 2. Conduct of life. I. Title.
BP605.N48R63   1994
299'.93—dc20   94-2565
                                              CIP

Artwork © 1994 by Elizabeth Jean Rogers

Printed in the United States of America

Llewellyn Publications
A Division of Llewellyn Worldwide, Ltd.
P.O. Box 64383, St. Paul, MN 55164-0383

Dedication

This book is dedicated to Mama and Daddy. Mama, your delight in many of these ideas encouraged me to write this book. May you continue to joyously awaken to your own power and to the love of the Universe for you.

This book is also dedicated to those of you who until this moment looked outside of yourselves for approval and truth. Uncover the wisdom, energy, and love of your higher Self and discover the peace and the joy for which you yearn.

Special Thanks

To Mary, Ruthie, Joyce, Gary, Wanda, Linda, Dinnie, Lynn, Debbie, Roz, and Rochelle: Your inspiring thoughts and/or editorial advice were essential to the writing of this book. The sharing of your ideas and time with me is deeply appreciated. Thank you for your enthusiasm, encouragement, and love.

To my husband Larry: Thank you for the computer expertise, tremendous support, and for loving me just the way I am.

To the authors, teachers, and guides who have helped me formulate my thoughts: You have brought me peace and an awareness of a richer, fuller existence. Thank you for the love and the joy you gently helped me discover.

To my granddaughter, Ashley Danielle: I feel an urgency as never before to "do it now." This book was finished in an effort to honor your short life. I love you. Thank you for sharing your love with me.

Contents

Preface

Experience this book during quiet moments with yourself—moments spent especially for you. Let this be a time to let go of the responsibilities of the day; a time for relaxation and reflection. Now is the time to accept your own inner wisdom and love; to discover the power of your thoughts and create a joyous life.

The chapters in this journal and guide have six parts: basic concepts, Quiet Reflection, Message From Within, Take Action, Burning Desire, and Affirmations.

The first pages of each chapter are the basic concepts of that section, describing vital methods of overcoming blocks that keep happiness from you. These startlingly simple ideas will help you create the joy you've always wanted in your life.

Quiet Reflection gently leads the way to a new, joyous life. The effective use of relaxation and guided visualization will enable you to join with the creative Energy of the Universe. These quiet moments will reward you with magnificent changes in your life and deep personal understanding and growth.

Message From Within shows you how to contact knowledge and inspiration from the truest part of yourself. You will learn to create a path to your own inner wisdom. Use this page to record your feelings and discoveries. Let this book become a personal expression of you!

Take Action is designed to help you become aware of your thoughts and feelings. It will help you replace destructive thoughts and behaviors with constructive ones. You will learn to direct your thoughts and take action to get what you want.

Burning Desire is a statement of what you intensely wish to create in your life; it is a dream you want to come true. Ideally it is a feeling, quality, or a life situation you want to develop rather than a possession you would like to acquire.

Affirmations can help you creatively define and fulfill your burning desires. An affirmation is a statement that asserts that what you want already exists in a perfect reality. It is written in such a way that it brings vivid images of success to mind and it produces strong feelings of pleasure and fulfillment. By developing and experiencing affirmations, you will quickly bring into your life your deepest desires and truest needs. Make your dreams reality!

Experience these chapters and find truth deep within your own heart. Rejoice in becoming one with the creative energy of the Universe. Learn to accept and love yourself and others. Overcome negativity and transform it into positive energy. Bring to yourself all that is yours by divine right for your greatest joy, for your highest good, and for the highest good of all. Think joyous thoughts, for what you think is what you get!

A Personal Note

When I was a little girl I thought that one day I would grow into perfection: a perfection of complete wisdom, happiness, and unconditional love. I was crushed when I lost hope of finding this perfect world. I felt betrayed; powerless; confused. My self-doubt paralyzed me.

After much searching, I discovered it was my choice to live in fear or to move forward. This book began as a letter to my mother, and became a journal to myself. It has been my way of dealing with my own fear.

This book contains the awareness I am beginning to discover. Life is a time to grow—a time to recognize myself and others as creations of inner wisdom and love. A time to contact the truth and creativity of my deepest Self; to experience pain and learn from my earthly trials; to understand and direct my emotions. A time to experience the joy of this moment. Hopefully, a time to release limitations through compassion, insight, and growth.

I am here to bring understanding and love into the Universe; to overcome my fear and hopefully give others the courage to overcome theirs, as well. I am at the dawn of a new awareness. I have just begun.

This life may not be where I learn to recognize complete perfection, but I will continue to reach for it. I have a long journey. As I make my way into the Light, I find the innocent little girl who believed in perfection touched truth as it is in eternity.

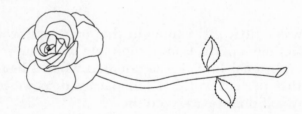

Celebrate Life

Listen to this moment;
It is the song of eternity.
Awaken to the here and now;
Delight in the wonder of living!

You choose your path in life;
Be alive each step of the way!
Your pain will lead you to growth;
Your thoughts will lead you to joy.

Feel free to follow your dreams;
Discover your life's perfect plan.
Listen to the gentle voice within you,
It whispers the truth of your soul.

Your peace draws your happiness near,
By your thoughts it is conceived;
By your actions it strengthens and grows;
By your love your happiness is born.

You are a child of the Universe,
A creation of wisdom and love.
You are divinely protected and guided
All the days of your precious life.

Celebrate life!
Peace, joy, and abundance overflow.
Magnificent love awaits you;
Accept it into your heart.

—Elizabeth J. Rogers

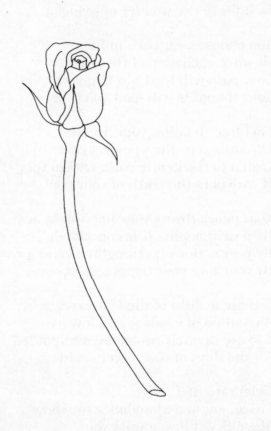

1

Feel the Power

We are all surrounded by eternity and united by love.
This is the one center from which all species issue, as
rays from a sun, and to which all species return.

—G. Bruno

Feel the Power

There is a Power* that is the essence of all that is. This Power is pure and unconditional Love; infinite Intelligence and Wisdom. It is Truth and Justice; perfect Order and Unity. It is Nature and the Laws of Nature. It is the Perfect Plan of all that exists. It is Harmony and Balance; Goodness and Light; Creativity and Inspiration. It has no beginning and no end. It is one with all you feel, touch, and see. It is one with your imagination and creativity. It is one with your body, mind, and spirit.

The Universe around you is pure energy. Light, sound, thought, and matter consist of this energy. You are a part of this energy and it is a part of you. Its power flows through you. It is the force inside you that is your life itself. It is one with your mind and the wisdom you hold in your deepest knowing.

Use your own intellect and inner wisdom to uncover the truth of your connection with the Power of the Universe. Discover your feelings and beliefs. No one but you is responsible for your life; no one but you can develop a relationship with a Higher Power. Deep within you is your connection to the Light—awaken to it and it will guide your way to truth.

Look to the wisdom of the ages for enlightenment. Discover the meaning behind the words of teachers and spiritual teachings; they hold inspiration and insight to awaken your own inner wisdom. Search for the messages that lie buried in your subconscious mind. Deep within your own heart lie answers that await your discovery.

There is an energy that is always available to you—open yourself to it. Allow it to unite with the highest part of yourself. Take a moment to be still, allow your mind to be quiet, and request the Power of the Universe to flow to you and fill you. Visualize a magnificent white Light descending upon

---

*We speak of this Power by many names. Some of these names are God; God the Father, Son, and Holy Spirit; Brahman; Aten; Allah; Yahweh; Great Mother; the Power of the Universe; the Divine Whole; the Universal Mind; the Higher Power; the Great Spirit; the Creator; and the Light. There are many more. If you like, substitute the name you prefer.

you, filling you with peace and creative energy. This peace will allow you to experience a new awareness of harmony and protection, and this energy will fill you with courage and vitality to take action. Delight in this connection with unlimited wisdom and infinite love. Call upon it any time, night or day. It waits for you tenderly and lovingly.

Feel the radiant energy of the Power inside you. You create your destiny with the power that flows through you. Let it lead you to your greatest joy and to your highest good, for the highest good of all.

You may sometimes feel scared and alone ... you are not alone! The Power of the Universe flows through you. Awaken your connection to this Power. You are divinely protected and guided on your journey into the Light.

Quiet Reflection

Create a mood of comfort and peace for yourself. Dim the lights, play soft music, burn a candle, or do whatever soothes you. Read each Quiet Reflection in this book once to yourself, then let your thoughts guide you through it once more. Feel free to change or embellish these Quiet Reflections. Let them stimulate your own creativity and develop them into meaningful growth experiences for you.

Sit or lie down with your spine straight, and get comfortable. Yawn and s t r e t c h; close your eyes. Breathe deeply and relax. Let all your muscles go limp while you go to a quiet place inside yourself. Keep breathing deeply and slowly. Count back from 10 to 1, relaxing more with each count. Visualize the following:

Imagine a beam of radiant white Light from the cosmos shining down upon you. Feel this brilliant beam of Energy enter through the top of your head and flow through every part of you. Feel Energy from deep within the earth surge upward and enter your body through your feet. This Energy flows up and out the top of your head. The Energy from the earth mixes harmoniously with the Energy from the cosmos. Feel the Energy-saturated Light continue to flow through you, penetrating every part of your body, mind, and spirit. You are perfectly connected with the Light, the Energy, and the Love of All That Is. Feel the Power inside you—feel the wisdom, the peace, and the harmony. Say to yourself, "The Power of the Universe flows through me. The Light is with me; I am the Light. I radiate this Light to the Universe around me for my good and for the highest good of all."

Enjoy this feeling of peace for as long as you wish. When you are ready, take a deep breath and begin to move your hands and feet. Stretch and open your eyes.

Message From Within

Experience each Message From Within after Quiet Reflection while you are still relaxed and open to messages of inner wisdom.

Don't think about what you are writing; just write. Don't worry about spelling or grammar. Don't stop writing once you start. Don't be afraid; just write whatever comes to mind.

Discover your connection with the Higher Power of the Universe. This Power exists in you as your truest Self. Recognize the truth of who you are. Open your heart and mind to the ideas that begin to flow, and write down the feelings and insights that come to you from your deepest knowing.

Take Action

Resist the urge to skip past this page! Answer these questions and take the first steps toward creating a new and joyous life.

In each Quiet Reflection you are asked to surround yourself with loving Energy and Light. When you visualize this Energy or Light you allow yourself to merge fully with the Higher Power of the Universe. When you feel your happiest, totally safe and most fulfilled, you have united with this Higher Power also.

Write down what brings you feelings of oneness with this Higher Power.

You can bring this strength and peace to yourself whenever you want. Take just a moment at different times today and ask for Light to fill you.

Burning Desire

I have a burning desire to feel the
Power of the Universe
flow through me.

Affirmations

Radiant Power fills me.
My total being overflows
with Light and Love!
The Infinite Wisdom of the Universe
surges through every part of me.
A wondrous journey is before me.
I am divinely protected and guided
on my journey into the Light.
I go forward with anticipation and joy.

My Personal Affirmations

Take a moment at the end of each chapter
to write your own personal affirmations.

2

Discover Your Higher Self

The finding of God is the coming to one's ownself.

—Meher Beba

Discover Your Higher Self

You are so much more than you think you are! Within you is the highest part of yourself. This Self is the way you truly are, in total perfection. It holds your own perfect inner beauty, wisdom, and love. Your higher Self is sometimes called the soul, the subconscious mind, or the deep Self. Your higher Self is your truest Self ... peaceful, natural, and strong.

The life force that flows within you is extremely powerful. It is the power that keeps your body functioning; the energy that keeps your blood flowing through your body and causes you to breathe. It is the energy that builds and repairs your body. It is the power that leads you to your highest good; that lets you feel your greatest joy. It is the happy, loving way you feel deep inside yourself. Your higher Self inspires you to grow, create, and love! This Self is your spiritual Self that exists forever; the real you lives on.

You are pure energy. This energy is your connection to the Divine Power of the Universe. This creative energy may not be visible to you, but it is very much a part of you. Awaken to your inner Self and you will begin to think, act, and feel whole, joyous, and alive!

Your higher Self communicates with you through your intuition and dreams. Accept your inner feelings of knowing without being aware of how you know. Begin to recall your dreams and see what meaning they hold for you. Have a notebook by your bed to jot down fleeting thoughts that might escape your memory when you become fully awake.

Messages from your higher Self sometimes come in unexpected ways. A song on the radio might awaken you to something that is necessary for you to understand. A passage from a book might say just what you need to grasp, or a friend might give you exactly the information you need at just the right time.

Be open to guidance from your higher Self. Ask for help and it will come. To contact your higher Self, search deep inside yourself for truth. Relax and become quiet ... just be. Ask for inspiration and information.

The still, quiet messages of your higher Self will come as thoughts, feelings, or images. You will receive powerful information and feel a thrilling awareness of harmony and truth. Open yourself to it and accept the true wisdom that flows from deep inside yourself.

Rely on your own inner guidance; discover your own power and inner perfection. You hold your life's perfect plan in your own heart. Find the truth of who you are. Discover your higher Self and awaken your connection with that genuine, beautiful being.

Quiet Reflection

Sit or lie down with your spine straight. Yawn and s t r e t c h. Close your eyes. Breathe deeply, relax, and let all your muscles go limp. Feel a stream of Light-filled Energy beaming down from the cosmos and flowing up from the earth. Let this Light flow harmoniously through your body, mind, and spirit, and radiate from every part of your being. Keep breathing deeply and slowly while you go to a quiet place inside yourself. Count back from 10 to 1, relaxing more with each deep breath. Visualize the following:

Imagine a delightful path that winds up a peaceful mountainside. As you explore this path to your higher Self, you are filled with joyous energy. Feel yourself walking up this path, drawn to the top as though a magnet is pulling you upward. In front of you appears a radiant crystal palace. Luminous and spectacular, it rises before you. It sparkles with rainbow fire from the Light that is streaming from it. In this palace you will experience the magnificence of your higher Self; discover your deepest joys and your highest good. You will always experience peace and complete protection here. All the knowledge you want will be revealed to you within these brilliant crystal walls. The doors burst open as you draw near and golden Light pours out to welcome you; you merge with this golden Light as you enter. Unconditional love fills you; deep peace comes upon you. Bask in this energy! Reach out and embrace this truest part of yourself; feel it embracing you. Let your own love fill you with joy. This inner source of energy and truth has been waiting for you to accept it all your life. It is with you always ... let yourself feel its presence at every moment. You are never alone. Enjoy the deep peace this acceptance brings.

Enjoy this feeling of peace for as long as you wish. When you are ready, take a deep breath and begin to move your hands and feet. Stretch and open your eyes.

Message From Within

This section in each chapter is an opportunity to develop a path to the wisdom buried deep inside you. Contact with your highest knowing becomes easier each time you try.

You may have once thought that the real you was confused, scared, and alone. That was only an illusion; a shadow that hid you from the truth of who you really are. Awaken to the reality of you! In quiet solitude, turn inward and contact your higher Self and the Energy that flows through you. Write down the insights, feelings, and images that come to you.

Take Action

Your higher Self gives you strong messages through your emotions and intuition. Become aware of your true feelings. When you feel confused and unhappy, your inner knowing is telling you to change. Trust in yourself and go a different way. When you feel happy, in balance, and alive, you are going in the right direction.

Using only positive words describe yourself at your very best, with all your good qualities and abilities.

Describe the activities you do or that you would like to do that bring you feelings of pure joy.

What will you do today to bring out the best in yourself and create more joy in your life?

Burning Desire

I have a burning desire to hear the
still, quiet voice of my higher Self.

Affirmations

I am connected with the Divine
Power of the Universe.
This Power flows through the
truest part of me, my higher Self.
My higher Self is my power,
my inner wisdom, truth, and beauty.
It speaks silently; I listen.
My right thoughts, right words, and
right actions are revealed to me.
Together we create a joyous future.

My Personal Affirmations

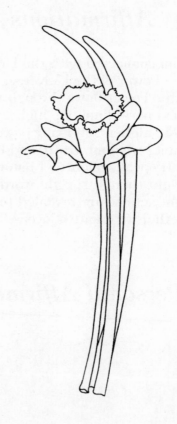

3

Breathe Deeply and Relax

E.J. Rogers

Rest is not idleness, and to lie sometimes on the grass under the trees on a summer's day, listening to the murmur of water, or watching the clouds float across the sky, is by no means a waste of time.

—Sir J. Lubbock

Breathe Deeply and Relax

You may often experience tension in your emotions, thoughts, or body. Sometimes you might hold back feelings or push yourself too hard, which may cause you to tighten your muscles and hold back your breathing. Breathing reflects how your body is reacting to a situation. If you direct your breathing, you can also gain control of how your body reacts. When you become tense, take a moment to relax and breathe deeply. This will improve your emotional level, your body's well-being, and your mental alertness.

Tension affects you physically, mentally, and emotionally. It often results in back, neck, and shoulder pain, upset stomach, headache, and other physical problems. It may cause fatigue, poor performance, frustration, and forgetfulness. Tension makes your body tighten and your muscles become exhausted.

Allow your body to relax—simply let your body go limp. Physically letting go also allows emotional and mental relaxation. Just becoming aware that a muscle is tense will often help it loosen and relax. Gently stretching a tight muscle can also relieve its tension.

The cells of the body need oxygen to release stored energy. Breathing brings in oxygen and gets rid of carbon dioxide. Allow your body to function effectively. Inhale deeply; use your lungs fully. Let your abdomen and then your upper chest fill with air. Exhale and let your chest and abdomen empty at the same time.

Breathing deeply and slowly can be used to energize as well as relax. Breathe in the breath of life and let energy and vitality flow through you. Relax and let your inner beauty glow. Breathe deeply and become refreshed, alert, and calm.

When you become angry or fearful, you are aware only of these feelings. Your breathing may become fast or may even be held back. Your body knows something is wrong. It reacts, and adrenalin is pumped through your system. Your heart beats faster and your body becomes tense and tight.

If you can simply remember to breathe you will take your focus away from your negative feelings. Remembering to breathe will bring you back to this moment and take your thoughts away from your fear or anger; it will allow you to think clearly and become calm, bringing your body back into its natural, relaxed state.

If your body performs properly, your mind operates at its best; therefore your body functions at its best. It is a cycle in which each directly affects the other.

Notice when you become tense and take a few moments to relax. Stretch and take a deep breath—just let go. Your ability to relax and breathe fully will bring you back into the present moment. It will restore your energy, improve your health, and give you deep peace of mind.

Quiet Reflection

Get in a comfortable position, either sitting or lying down. Your spine is straight and your legs are uncrossed. If you are sitting, your feet are flat on the floor and your hands rest easily in your lap. If you are lying down, your arms are comfortably at your sides. You may wish to put a pillow under your legs if that is comfortable for you. Yawn and s t r e t c h. Close your eyes. Breathe deeply, relax, and let all your muscles go limp while you go to a quiet place inside yourself. Surround yourself with loving energy. Keep breathing deeply and slowly. Count back from 10 to 1, relaxing more with each count. Visualize the following:

Go within. Perhaps you are inside your crystal palace*, or outside in one of its lovely gardens. Relax and get comfortable with your surroundings. Breathe in the fresh, sweet air. Feel the welcoming energy that waits for you here. Surround yourself with protective white Light. Breathe in and let it fill you.

Take a deep breath. Yawn. Fill up your whole chest with this magnificent Light-filled energy. Stretch and tense your whole body. Continue to yawn and stretch for as long as you can. Now exhale and relax completely.

Continue to exhale deeply. Pull in your abdomen and push out all the air from your lungs. To the count of four, inhale a Light-filled breath of air through your nose. Push your abdomen all the way out with air, them fill your upper chest. Keeping your chest full of air, lift your shoulders up and back. Slowly exhale to the count of four. Let your chest and abdomen sink down together. Exhale completely; pull in your abdomen and push all the air out. Totally relax.

---

*Create a retreat of your own—it can be made of jewels or rough-hewn logs. Visualize whatever lets you feel safe and joyous whenever you come to this quiet place inside yourself.

Feel protective white Light gently kiss your forehead. A wave of peace spreads over you; you are perfectly safe. The Light softly touches your eyelids, and the muscles around your eyes relax. Continue breathing deeply and slowly. The Light comforts your cheeks, jaw, and tongue. Your whole head is relaxed. The calming Light fills your neck, shoulders, and upper back muscles; they go totally limp. The Light soothes your arms and your hands. Tranquility flows through you. The Light enters your chest and your stomach. As the Light radiates through you, your internal organs and glands relax to their natural state. The Light gently touches your lower back and hips. You float on a cloud of relaxation ... all is well. The Light fills your thighs, knees, and calves. You feel as light as air. The Light kisses your toes. Your feet and ankles relax and become warm. Your whole body is floating; you are completely relaxed. Let the peace of the Universe flow through you and fill you with joy.

Enjoy this feeling of peace for as long as you wish. When you are ready, take a deep breath and begin to move your hands and feet. Stretch and open your eyes.

Message From Within

You deserve this quiet time for yourself. Let go of all pressure and obligations. Relax, breathe deeply, and bring into your mind's eye that which you want to understand. Be open to the powerful answers that flow to you from your deepest knowing. Write down all that comes to you.

Take Action

Notice when you become tense or upset during the day. Write down what made you feel this way. Note where you felt tension or unease in your body.

When you become tense or upset, take a few moments for yourself. Stretch and take a few deep breaths. Bring yourself back to the present moment and become calm, refreshed, and relaxed.

Special Note: If you have not touched your pen to this book yet, ask yourself why. The written word is powerful. Write in this book now!

Burning Desire

I have a burning desire
to easily and completely relax.

Affirmations

As I inhale deeply,
I breathe in Light-filled energy.
As I exhale, all tension flows out.
I am nourished by healing energy.
I allow all tightness to lift away.
I am pleasantly relaxed;
my mind is clear.
I am filled with peace.

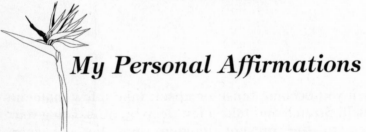

My Personal Affirmations

4

The Joy of Meditation

E.J.Rogers

True silence is the rest of the mind; it is to the spirit what sleep is to the body, nourishment and refreshment.

—William Penn

The Joy of Meditation

Meditation brings forth tremendous growth and a profound change for the better. Meditation allows you to experience relaxation, freedom from stress, and personal joy. Meditation quiets the mind and revives the body. It is a restful time for yourself; a time to discover your own highest wisdom. A time to become still and just *be*. A time to feel deep inner peace and experience the calm; the quiet.

There is more than one way to meditate. There is no pressure to do it the "right" way. Its benefits cannot be forced. Go at your own speed with no expectations of what should happen. With just doing it, the rewards will come.

Begin with a feeling of openness and a desire to grow. Discover the highest part of yourself that is complete, natural, loving, and free. Deep inside your own heart lie the answers you desire. Open yourself to them.

Your inner guidance comes in silent awareness. You will not "hear voices," but you will discover inner knowing that fills you with a wave of truth and harmony.

You may receive answers in symbols or images that do not have an obvious meaning for you. Allow yourself to interpret them in a way that feels right to you. If their meaning does not become clear, look to your innermost knowing for more information.

Sometimes during meditation you may experience powerful emotions. You may uncover a truth or feeling that is painful. Go with these feelings and learn what they have to teach you. Allow yourself to release the pain. Cry if you want—tears are cleansing.

When you are ready to meditate, go to a quiet place where you can relax and remain uninterrupted. Unplug the phone and close the door. The room temperature should not be too warm or too cool, but have a blanket close by in case you become chilly. Take off your shoes and jewelry, and wear loose clothing of natural fibers so that you will be as comfortable as possible.

Create an atmosphere of calm and harmony for yourself. Turn down the lights; perhaps light a candle. Turn on soft music. Involve all your senses when meditating. Have a favorite fragrance in the room such as a scented candle, incense, a sprig of pine, cinnamon, or a delicate perfume.

Meditation can be done with eyes open or closed. You may wish to keep your eyes open and focused on an object such as a flickering candle, or you may find that closing your eyes and concentrating on an image, thought, sound, or object works best for you. You may decide to concentrate on your breathing, either with your eyes open or your eyes closed. Experiment and find what helps you clear your mind of distractions.

Sit or lie down with your arms and legs uncrossed. You can be in a chair, on the floor, in bed, or wherever you feel comfortable.

Use the Quiet Reflection in each chapter as a guide to begin meditating. You will be asked to go to the crystal palace you have created in your imagination. Feel free to create your own special retreat. Whenever you bring your thoughts here you will experience being in a state of harmony, serene and complete. Enjoy the quiet; the peace. Become centered and balanced in mind, body, and spirit. Discover your highest Self. Experience your connection with life. Feel your unity with the world in which you live. Meditate and become one with the Universe—feel the power; the total acceptance and unconditional love. You are not alone.

Quiet Reflection

Sit or lie down with your spine straight. Yawn and s t r e t c h. Close your eyes. Breathe deeply, relax, and let all your muscles go limp. Feel a stream of Light-filled Energy beaming down from the cosmos and flowing up from the earth. Let this Light flow harmoniously through your body, mind, and spirit, and radiate from every part of your being. Keep breathing deeply and slowly while you go to a quiet place inside yourself. Count back from 10 to 1, relaxing more with each deep breath. Visualize the following:

Allow your surroundings to fade into the background. Go once more to the crystal palace you have created in your imagination. Select a lovely, tranquil area on the grounds. This spot is safe and protected; you can be totally at ease and fully relaxed here. Breathe in ... Out. Relax and get comfortable. Concentrate on your breathing and become relaxed. In ... Out. Your thoughts will not have room for fear, anger, or stress. In ... Out. You have left your obligations behind. You deserve this special time for yourself. In ... Out.

Clear your mind of logical thoughts. To help you do this, focus on your breathing. In ... Out. If distracting thoughts come to mind, tenderly let them go and gently bring your mind back to your breathing and the words "In" and "Out."

Your mind focuses only on your breathing. In ... Out. Breathe through your nose. In ... Out. Make the outward breath as long as the inward breath. In ... Out. Continue to breathe deeply without irregularities. In ... Out ... In ... Out ... In ... Out ... In ... Out ... In ... Out ... In ... Out ...

Continue to breathe and enjoy this feeling of peace for as long as you wish. When you are ready, begin to move your hands and feet. Stretch and open your eyes.

Message From Within

Experience Message From Within while you are still in a receptive state. Pick up your pencil and write as fast as you can. You may find yourself writing more poetically than you normally would. You may wonder where these profound words originate—they come from you! Discover the innocence of your inner child; benefit from the wisdom of your inner sage. Write down whatever comes to mind.

Take Action

How often do you take time for yourself and allow yourself to relax?

How might taking the time to relax benefit you?

How might taking the time to relax benefit those around you?

When was the last time you felt total relaxed, totally at peace with yourself and the Universe?

Burning Desire

I have a burning desire to
experience deep peace and
awaken my highest wisdom.

Affirmations

I deserve special moments for myself.
During this quiet time I contact inner wisdom.
It speaks; I listen.
I connect with my highest creativity.
I find my connection to all of creation.
The harmony and peace I experience
remain with me throughout my everyday life.

My Personal Affirmations

5

Think Constructive Thoughts

E. Rogers

*Cherish your visions; cherish your ideals; cherish the
music that stirs in your heart, the beauty that forms
in your mind, the loveliness that drapes your purest
thoughts, for out of them will grow all delightful conditions, all heavenly environment; of these, if you but
remain true to them, your world will at last be built.*

—James Allen

Think Constructive Thoughts

Your thoughts create your present and your future; all that you create or achieve begins with a thought. Responsibility for your thoughts and your feelings is yours. You, and only you, create your thoughts. They do not develop on their own. They are not formed by what occurs in your life or by other people. You form your thoughts inside your mind.

You developed your pattern of thinking; you formed it and you can change it. Decide if you want your thought patterns to support or destroy you. You are in charge.

Examine your thoughts. Do you see a pattern of harmful, destructive thoughts? Learn to become aware of gloomy, damaging thoughts. Become conscious of your thoughts and you can begin to reform your thought patterns.

Change the way you think, and you change the way you feel and act. All change starts from your thoughts and then shows in your feelings and actions. Learn to direct your thoughts and you gain control of your life; improve your thoughts and you enrich your life.

Let go of thoughts that destroy you and rob you of the joy you deserve. Don't waste time and energy on thoughts that aren't for your highest good. Get rid of thoughts that don't help you in the present.

Taking any new action may seem difficult at first, but you can do it if you only keep trying. Your desire for a joyous life will help you. Old thought habits can be changed with a burning desire to do so.

Don't force change, allow it. Allow yourself to let go of past thinking habits. If thoughts that harm you enter your mind, gently let them go. Turn them around and create productive thoughts. Stop your negative thoughts and replace them with energetic thoughts. Constructive, powerful thoughts don't just happen, you create them!

Develop a pattern of creating supportive and optimistic thoughts. If you sincerely desire to be calm, centered, and content, begin now to form new thought patterns that allow this.

Allow yourself to develop loving thoughts regarding yourself, others, and the world around you. Focus on joyous feelings you wish to experience. You will bring these feelings into your life by just remembering to create optimistic, constructive thoughts.

No amount of positive thinking will keep pain and challenges from entering your life, but *you* direct your thoughts and the way you react to them. Look at a troublesome circumstance as an opportunity to develop control over your emotions and thoughts. Respond to difficulties with a compassionate and optimistic attitude, and loving feelings and energy will surround you.

Do not let outer circumstances dictate how you feel and what you think inside. Will you think a situation is unbearable, that you cannot go on, or will you look for a solution and find a way through it?

Learn from each painful occurrence in your life. Ask yourself, "What response will best serve me?" Turn an unpleasant situation into one that benefits you. Create good because of it. This will put you back in control and enable you to constructively focus on achieving your goal.

Your thoughts influence your responses to the people in your life. If someone acts in a way that would normally irritate you, will you allow them to control your thoughts and emotions? Will you give your power to them? Will you ruin this fine moment in time? Or will you take a deep breath and think, "I am protected; I am calm. I direct my thoughts and I choose to remain detached and undisturbed by this"? Create thoughts that allow you to remain clearheaded, energetic, and able to perform at your best.

It is difficult to take positive action if your thoughts focus on past disappointments and harsh feelings. You might remember only the painful feelings from the past. You may have received support and nurturing but it may not stand out in your mind.

Try to recall the good in your past experiences. Allow happy memories to surface. No matter what your past, you are in charge of your life now. Take responsibility for your feelings. Discover your ability to forgive, and get involved with the enjoyment of the present! Allow yourself to let go of the past and create peace for yourself in this moment.

Think constructive, joyous thoughts and you will create a joyous and fulfilling life. It is impossible to attract good into your life if you focus on what terrible occurrence might await you. Don't picture frightening experiences entering your life, but focus on the abundance and beauty that is available to you at this very moment. Opportunities and joy are plentiful in the Universe. Accept your gift of life with delight.

Your thoughts can be used against you or to support you. Use the magnificent power of your thoughts to create the peace and happiness for which you yearn. What do you want to experience each moment of your life? Pleasure and harmony or pain and confusion? It is your choice.

It is a challenge to actively redirect your thought patterns. You can do it! Focus on positive actions that you will take and allow refreshing ideas and supportive beliefs to form in your mind. Focus on the delight your new thought patterns will bring; focus on how you want to feel.

If you find yourself slipping back into destructive thought patterns, try again. Stop those thoughts and affirm your desire to think constructive thoughts so that you can feel good.

Beginning now, create optimistic, constructive thoughts. Think good thoughts and you will bring good into your life. Think loving thoughts and you will be surrounded with love. Think positive thoughts and positive things will happen. Your productive, loving thoughts surround you with harmonious energy. Delight in the pleasure your new thought patterns create for you.

Your thoughts are energy. The power of your mind attracts what is needed to fulfill your desires. Request that your highest good enter your life. Picture your life as you want it to be and it will be drawn to you. To achieve what you want, focus on what you desire as though it is already accomplished. What you see in your mind, you create and make a reality. Join with the powerful energy of the Universe and allow your highest good to enter your life.

With the magnificent power of your thoughts you can create joy in your present and future. Form your thoughts with care—what you think is what you get!

Quiet Reflection

Sit or lie down with your spine straight. Yawn and s t r e t c h. Close your eyes. Breathe deeply, relax, and let all your muscles go limp. Feel a stream of Light-filled Energy beaming down from the cosmos and flowing up from the earth. Let this Light flow harmoniously through your body, mind, and spirit, and radiate from every part of your being. Keep breathing deeply and slowly while you go to a quiet place inside yourself. Count back from 10 to 1, relaxing more with each deep breath. Visualize the following:

Travel once more up the path to the crystal palace of Light you have created. When you come to this special place, it is safe to face your innermost feelings. Here you can learn to let go of destructive thoughts. Go to a protected spot on your crystal palace grounds and allow your negative thoughts to surface so that you can let them go forever. Picture these negative thoughts as a swirling mist of confusion inside your body. Eliminate this confusion! Acknowledge it and allow it to leave. Pull it out from deep inside you. Feel this confusion gently lifting from your body, easily and completely. Gently, gently, all traces of this negativity leave you ... now it is totally gone. See it outside your body, floating away from you.

    Your crystal palace holds all your goodness and love. Everything you ever wanted lies waiting for you in your crystal palace. Take as much time as you like to explore your dreams. See them easily coming true for you. Continue to allow new, lighthearted thoughts to surface. Experience the pleasure you can create at any time, in any place, just by creating a joyous thought. Enjoy the success and happiness this newfound treasure brings. Delight in the joy of your imagination!

Enjoy this feeling of peace for as long as you wish. When you are ready, take a deep breath and begin to move your hands and feet. Stretch and open your eyes.

Message From Within

Your higher Self is not a strange, unreachable being. Contact with your own perfect inner wisdom and love comes naturally with true desire. Relax, be still, and open yourself to loving thoughts of inspiration. Write down everything that flows to you.

Take Action

Become aware of the thoughts you think and you will become able to direct them. For one day (or just one hour) note every negative thought that you notice yourself thinking.

With awareness and desire you can change your thoughts. Rewrite the most common negative thoughts you listed above into positive statements.

Carry these constructive thoughts with you. When you find yourself thinking destructively, read this list. Begin thinking these positive, loving thoughts and you will change your life!

Burning Desire

I have a burning desire to use my thoughts
to create a joyous life.

Affirmations

I alone create my thoughts.
I now choose thoughts that fill
me with positive, joyous feelings.
My thoughts create peace and
happiness for me.
My thoughts go before me and pave my
way with love and joy.
Together we sweep away
all obstacles in my path.
I use the powerful energy of my
thoughts for the highest good of all.

My Personal Affirmations

6

Experience Affirmations

If one advances confidently in the direction of his dreams, and endeavors to live the life which he has imagined, he will meet with a success unexpected in common hours.

—Henry David Thoreau

Experience Affirmations

An affirmation is a positive statement that what you deeply desire is already so. What you see in your imagination is as real as anything you can touch right now. A written and frequently visualized affirmation attracts to it what it needs to materialize, if you believe you can attain it.

Affirmations are powerful. You will create what you continue to affirm and visualize (or something even better!). Affirmations help you replace old, useless thought patterns with powerful, constructive ones. They can help you dramatically change your life.

The words you say and the thoughts you hold in your imagination are creative energy in action. They create your present and your future. Speak constructively and visualize positive life situations and you will create a joyous life. You will create and attract to you that which you think about repeatedly. The more energy you give a thought, the faster it will come into being.

Create your affirmations from the desires of your heart and your truest needs. Visualize your life as you would like it to be. What feelings would you experience if your life were just as you wanted right now? Write down these feelings.

You may wish to bring objects into your life—a new car, clothes, etc. How would having these possessions make you feel? Confident? Secure? Happy? Aren't these feelings your true desire? Having the possessions without the pleasurable feelings would be useless, wouldn't it? So the feelings are what you truly want to attain.

Write an affirmation stating that you now have these feelings. Allow yourself to experience these emotions in your mind. You can, with practice, create these thoughts and feelings.

Later you will begin to bring objects into your life with the use of affirmations and the power of your mind.

Create your own affirmations. Write the affirmation in a way that states you already feel the positive, constructive emotions that you wish to experience.

An effective affirmation is written as a brief positive statement that what you deeply desire is now a reality (even if it is not yet physically so). Example: "I am now vibrantly healthy and feel good all over!" not "I don't feel pain in my body."

An affirmation is written in the present tense, as if the achievement is now a reality. Example: "I am confident and secure," not "I will soon become confident and secure."

An affirmation brings to mind vivid details of your accomplished goal. Example: "I dance with graceful ease and joyous mobility," not "I dance well."

An affirmation causes strong emotions of delight and success. Example: "I am filled with joy and anticipation as I greet my workday each morning," not "I am grateful I have a job."

An affirmation fills you with a burning desire that you firmly believe you will achieve. Example: "I trust in an abundant Universe and I easily pay my bills," not "I have one million dollars in the bank" (one day you may be able to affirm this, but you probably don't believe you could achieve this right now or you wouldn't be reading this book!).

Write your own personal affirmations and carry them with you. Read them in the morning when you wake up, and in the evening before you go to sleep. Read them to redirect your thoughts when you find yourself thinking negatively. Read them when you're waiting in line; when you're at a stoplight; when you're brushing your teeth. Read them often and whenever you like.

An effective affirmation arouses clear images of positive actions and results when you read it. When visualized, it fills you with powerful creative energy. Read your affirmation to begin the visualization process. Because you create what you see in your mind, see your goal as already accomplished. See your fulfilled desire in every detail. Experience where you are, who is there, and what is happening. Experience intense emotions of joy and success.

Experience your affirmation several times a day until it shows itself in your life. Focus on only positive thoughts and feelings during this process. If negative thoughts come to mind, gently let them fade away. Redirect your thoughts toward constructive ones. Visualize clearly what you want as if it is now a reality. You can see it, touch it, smell it—you can really experience it. Picture every detail and give it life! Feel deep emotions of success and joy. Give your desire positive, radiant energy.

Believe that your affirmation will come into your life. Your higher Self will bring to you anything you imagine if you believe that it is yours. The Universe holds an abundant supply of everything and wants you to enjoy your life. Give thanks to the power of the Universe. Let the joy of appreciation surge through your body, mind, and spirit.

When you see one of your affirmations fulfilled, create a new one. Use this process throughout your life to discover the happiness that belongs to you.

Trust that your highest good will come to you. Your desire is a reality in Universal intelligence. Keep the belief that your desire now belongs to you; believe even if there is no evidence that it is so. When you believe, you let go of barriers of negativity. Believe in your good and let go of fear, lack, limitation, pain, and disharmony. Change destructive thoughts and feelings into positive ones.

You will be delighted with the joy your affirmations and new thought patterns bring. Experience the rewards of affirmations and delight in the power of your thoughts!

Take Action

What life experiences or living conditions would you like to create?

What are the positive feelings you would have if you create these experiences or conditions in your life?

What could you do to experience these pleasurable feelings right now?

What are the five most important emotions or feelings that you want in your life?

What could bring you these feelings right now?

What behaviors, qualities, or attitudes do you wish to develop in yourself?

Use your above lists as a guide to create your own affirmations on the following pages.

Create Your Affirmations

There are five keys to creating an effective affirmation:

1. It is written as a brief positive statement that what you deeply desire is now so (even though it is not yet physically so).

2. It is written in the present tense, as if your affirmation is now a reality.

3. It brings to mind vivid details of your accomplished goal.

4. It causes strong emotions of delight and success.

5. It fills you with a burning desire you firmly believe you will achieve.

Message From Within

Let go of the pressures and tensions of the day and take some time to dream about how you want your life to be. Let creativity flow from deep inside you. Create your affirmations below the sample affirmations. Write down the ideas that flow to you from your inner wisdom.

Spiritual: I am divinely protected and guided all the moments of my precious life. This moment finds me filled with energy, wisdom, and love.

My Affirmation:

Personal: I love and accept myself. The truth of all I need to know flows to me from deep inside my highest knowing.

My Affirmation:

Family: I show my love and respect for each member of my family. I show each one how s/he is special to me.

My Affirmation:

Past: I let go of all the pain from my past. I am willing to for-give myself and everyone who has brought me pain.

My Affirmation:

Emotions: I am compassionate toward others' negativity and shortcomings. I surround myself with protective energy. I remain calm, clear-headed, and unharmed.

My Affirmation:

Physical/Mental Health: I release all negativity and pain from my mind, body, and spirit. Divine love and healing Light flow through me.

My Affirmation:

Education/Growth: I am alert; I learn quickly and remember information with ease. I express myself well on paper and when speaking.

My Affirmation:

Work: I easily discover the most important action to take and I complete it with confidence and ease. Doors of opportunity constantly swing open; success and abundance are mine.

My Affirmation:

Present Moment: I am fully aware of what I am doing in the present moment. I am glad to be alive in this magnificent Universe!

My Affirmation:

Positive Attitude: I find the good in every person, situation, and event. My attitude is positive and my thoughts are constructive.

My Affirmation:

Social: I smile and the world smiles back at me! My smile sends out loving, positive energy to the whole Universe.

My Affirmation:

Abundance: I create what is for my highest good. I have a plan of action. I believe that (my truest desire) is now on its way to me and will arrive on or before (date).

My Plan of Action:

My Affirmation:

Cut out the affirmation cards on the following pages and write your own personal affirmations on them. Carry the cards with you and experience them often.

My Personal Affirmation

My Personal Affirmation

My Personal Affirmation

My Personal Affirmation

My Personal Affirmation

My Personal Affirmation

My Personal Affirmation

My Personal Affirmation

My Personal Affirmation

My Personal Affirmation

My Personal Affirmation

My Personal Affirmation

Experience Your Affirmations

There are five keys to experiencing your affirmations:

1. Read the affirmation several times a day until it shows itself in your life.

2. Focus on positive thoughts and feelings during this process.

3. Visualize clearly what you want as if it is now achieved. Picture every detail and give it life!

4. Feel deep emotions of success and joy to give your desire positive, radiant energy.

5. Believe your affirmation will come into your life.

Quiet Reflection

Take the time to experience your own affirmations. Create the joy that belongs to you!

Have your affirmations with you now. Sit or lie down with your spine straight. Yawn and s t r e t c h. Close your eyes. Breathe deeply, relax, and let all your muscles go limp. Feel a stream of Light-filled Energy beaming down from the cosmos and flowing up from the earth. Let this Light flow harmoniously through your body, mind, and spirit, and radiate from every part of your being. Keep breathing deeply and slowly while you go to a quiet place inside yourself. Count back from 10 to 1, relaxing more with each deep breath. Visualize the following:

The wisdom, love, and harmony you experience in your imagination is your higher Self contacting you. You can create all you imagine. Your inner power and creativity wait for you. Let your thoughts draw to you the joy that is rightfully yours. Say your affirmation to yourself and experience it as a reality in your mind. Take some time and live every blissful detail. Give your affirmation powerful, positive energy. Let your energy join with the power of the Universe that flows to you upon your request. Imagine your affirmation floating out into the Universe, growing larger and larger. Surround it with Light and Energy in your mind's eye, and see it get brighter and brighter. Imagine that it continues to collect Energy as it draws what it needs to come into your life. Be at peace; your highest good is on its way to you.

Enjoy this feeling of peace for as long as you wish. When you are ready, take a deep breath and begin to move your hands and feet. Stretch and open your eyes.

7

Turn Fear Into Confidence

Do the thing you are afraid to do, and the death of fear is certain.

—Ralph Waldo Emerson

Turn Fear Into Confidence

Fear is often a negative illusion you create in the absence of self-love and inner listening. Imagined fear is disbelief in your own power. Unrealistic fear is the turning away from the reality of a loving and abundant Universe.

Face fear and it will go; run from fear and it will run after you. Determine if the fear is valid*—if you decide it is not, let the fear leave you. Acknowledge fear in the safety of your thoughts as soon as it is present. Uncover why you are afraid. Look inside yourself for truth. Question your fear and learn from the lessons it holds.

Fear is the root of all negativity. Do not dwell on negative thoughts and waste your energy on them, but acknowledge them and choose to let those negative feelings go. Deal with fear through understanding and compassion for yourself. Join with the unlimited Energy of the Universe for strength, and surround every aspect of this fear with unconditional love and understanding until it is gone.

You choose the way you want to feel; accept responsibility for your emotions. If you want to feel positive and confident, you can. You create what you experience in your imagination. Whatever your invalid fear says to you, say to yourself the exact opposite. If fear says you can't handle a situation, tell yourself you can easily manage it. Visualize a positive outcome. If fear threatens you with loss or lack, affirm your trust in a safe and abundant Universe and imagine more good coming into your life. Each time you face fear you will gain courage; each time it will become easier. You have the power to do what you want to do with confidence!

---

*If your fear is valid, take action! Remove yourself from danger and seek help. Develop a plan to neutralize the situation. This chapter concerns fear that does not find you in real danger.

Quiet Reflection

Sit or lie down with your spine straight. Yawn and s t r e t c h. Close your eyes. Breathe deeply, relax, and let all your muscles go limp. Feel a stream of Light-filled Energy beaming down from the cosmos and flowing up from the earth. Let this Light flow harmoniously through your body, mind, and spirit, and radiate from every part of your being. Keep breathing deeply and slowly while you go to a quiet place inside yourself. Count back from 10 to 1, relaxing more with each deep breath. Visualize the following:

Go to a beautiful waterfall near your crystal palace. Walk beneath this stream of sparkling, healing water, and experience the strength and love that flows from it into you. You feel no discomfort, only cleansing, energizing power. Feel this stream of clear, purifying water enter your body through the top of your head. Feel your own awakening as this refreshing water flows through you, cleansing you of all your fear. It energizes you and makes you strong. You are alive and joyous. Picture an opening in your feet where the water can escape. Let the water and your fear flow from your feet into the rushing stream where it is cleansed. Continue to feel cleansing water flowing in through the top of your head, through your body, and away with the bubbling current. This water reveals your inner strength, wisdom, and love. Feel the totality of your being. You are a perfect expression of the Universe. Your body, mind, and spirit are one; you are one with the Divine Whole. Feel the Power inside you! You are as clean and fearless as the first rainfall upon the earth ... sweet, fresh, and new. You are strong and confident. All you need to know is revealed to you.

Enjoy this feeling of peace for as long as you wish. When you are ready, take a deep breath and begin to move your hands and feet. Stretch and open your eyes.

Message From Within

Bring to mind your largest fear. What do you need to know about this fear? Be open to inspiration from your higher Self. Write down thoughts, images, and feelings that flow to you from your deepest knowing.

Take Action

List a situation, activity, or person you fear. When was the first time this fear came?

Do you have a genuine reason to now have this fear? Why or why not?

What are the problems of having this fear?

What feelings and actions would you like to experience instead of fear?

What will you do to replace this fear with confidence?

Burning Desire

I have a burning desire to turn fear
into confidence.

Affirmations

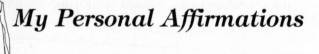

I request the powerful energy
of the Universe to fill me.
I face fears in the safety
of my thoughts.
I soothe my fear with compassion
and understanding.
I see myself performing with confidence.
I let fear flow away from me.
I am strong and powerful;
strength and confidence are mine.

My Personal Affirmations

8

Be Free of Old Habits

E.J. Rogers

He who gains victory over other men is strong; but he who gains victory over himself is all powerful.

—Lao-Tse

Be Free of Old Habits

You have formed habits in your life that you feel compelled to continue to maintain a state of well-being. Without performing these routines you may become restless, irritable, or anxious. You may even have to face withdrawal symptoms. These habits may include abusing alcohol, cigarettes, food, or drugs; excessive television viewing, reckless driving, gambling, nail biting ... the list is endless.

When should a habit be changed? If it damages your health, hurts you financially, or keeps you from functioning at your best. Change an old habit if it keeps you from achieving your goals and pursuing your heart's desire, makes you experience destructive emotions, or hides your genuine needs. In general, change a habit if it harms yourself or others.

If you find you are participating in habits that you no longer find useful or that bring you or others harm, you can let them go. Get outside support for things to which you are physically or psychologically addicted, but begin now to develop emotional and mental support for your change in behavior.

When you have excuses for continuing old habits, you don't see the truth. Find the hidden truth about your behavior and you may be better able to let it go. For each unwanted habit find the real reason you perpetuate it. To relax? To make you feel wanted? To temporarily escape from your problems or pain? How does it soothe you? What pleasure does it bring?

Do you perform this habit to make you feel "grown up" or part of a group? It is to hide or run away from your true feelings? Perhaps you use it as a way to be your own person; to go against society and your family and say, "I do what I want, no one controls me." Do you have hidden anger toward people you feel are trying to control you? Discover if you feel this habit is protecting you in some way.

Are the reasons you started this habit valid today? Whatever the reasons you started, now you have reasons that you continue. You feel it is in your best interest to continue or you would stop. Is this habit in your best interest? What brings about the desire to perform this habit? What are the reasons you still take this action today? How does it comfort you? Is it truly a valid way to fulfill your needs now?

Perhaps your habit gives you some sort of pleasure now, but what about over time? Does this habit truly serve you? How long will it benefit you? What are the advantages in relation to negative results? Will it cause more problems than it solves?

What is the hidden desire you are trying to fulfill? Go deep inside yourself to find the underlying desire you are attempting to satisfy. Discover what you really want, and learn to satisfy your needs in a way that is appropriate for you.

Now that the reasons you perform this habit are no longer hidden, it doesn't have such a hold on you. You can develop new, supportive patterns of behavior. Direct your feelings instead of relying on old habits. You control your thoughts and actions; replace old habits with positive, creative actions that support instead of destroy you.

Intellectually you may realize what the correct action is, but this does not guarantee that the correct action will be taken. You act in ways that you wish, not in ways that you think you should. You will not change your actions by force of will. Willpower might work for a short time, but not for long.

To make a permanent change in your behavior, learn to feel good about the change. What is for your highest good? Focus on the pleasure that the change will bring you. In fact, this new pleasure must be stronger than the pleasure the old habit now brings you.

Develop a burning desire to change; get emotionally involved. Vividly imagine the joy you will experience if you make this change. What can you accomplish if you change your behavior? How will you feel after you have triumphed? How will letting it go allow you to give and receive more affection? How will it let you grow? How will you profit if you change your behavior? Be creative! List every benefit you can imagine.

Develop a plan to erase unwanted habits from your life. What would satisfy your needs in a constructive, supportive way? What can you do to give yourself the genuine comfort for which you long?

Write down what you will do in order to change your behavior patterns. Put deadlines for when each action will occur.

Learn to take direct action instead of turning to your old habit. Keep trying different approaches, and see how each new action feels. Don't give up. Delight in the joy and pleasure these new actions bring you.

Your thoughts are powerful. Continue to focus on the joy of your newfound behavior. You create your thoughts and your actions. Enjoy being who you want to be!

Quiet Reflection

Sit or lie down with your spine straight. Yawn and s t r e t c h. Close your eyes. Breathe deeply, relax, and let all your muscles go limp. Feel a stream of Light-filled Energy beaming down from the cosmos and flowing up from the earth. Let this Light flow harmoniously through your body, mind, and spirit, and radiate from every part of your being. Keep breathing deeply and slowly while you go to a quiet place inside yourself. Count back from 10 to 1, relaxing more with each deep breath. Visualize the following:

Go to your crystal palace and experience yourself in your highest perfection, free of addictions and old habits. Here you can create new patterns that support you in your experience of life.

Walk through the rooms of your crystal palace. As you enter each door, visualize the new experiences you want in your life. See and feel them ... hear, smell, taste, and touch them. Join the power of your higher Self with the power of the Universe.

Doors to new lands, new peoples, and new ideals are opened here. Through each door lies a different pleasure; each room holds an exciting experience that fills you with satisfaction and self-worth. Explore your crystal palace. Delight in the secrets and love it holds for you.

This special place in your imagination is very powerful; it draws to you like a magnet whatever you desire. Come here often to relax, play, and build your dreams. Come here to experience yourself in your highest glory. Experience your dreams of how you wish your life to be, and give these dreams life!

Enjoy this peace for as long as you wish. When you are ready, take a deep breath and begin to move your hands and feet. Stretch and open your eyes.

Message from Within

Go deep inside yourself. Free your mind of shoulds and should nots. What is for your highest good concerning this habit? Write all that flows to you.

Take Action

What habit do you wish to break?

What good does this habit bring you? What are the reasons you perform this habit?

List all the reasons it is not in your best interest to continue this habit.

List all the benefits of ending this habit.

What is the hidden desire you are trying to fulfill with this habit?

What will satisfy your underlying desire?

What actions can you take to let this habit go?

Imagine you are free of this unwanted habit. Write affirmations of how you act and the pleasure that you experience now that this habit no longer controls you. Use only positive words in the present tense as if you are now free of this habit.

Experience your affirmations and visualize yourself enjoying a life free from the old habit. You control your life. Enjoy!

Burning Desire

I have a burning desire to be free of old habits
that are not for my highest good.

Affirmations

I face my feelings and desires
with compassion and understanding.
I find and experience valid ways
to comfort myself.
I love and respect myself.
I act in ways that are for my highest good
and that support my well-being.
I focus on the pleasure I enjoy
because I am free of this limiting habit.
I delight in the joy my new freedom gives me.

My Personal Affirmations

9

Take Action!

Joy is a feeling we can feel no matter what else is going on. The way to create joy is to do things joyfully. It's one of the easiest feelings to create. We need only remember to create it.

—John-Roger and Peter McWilliams

Take Action!

Have the courage to participate in new activities. This might be speaking to someone you don't know well, or it could be playing a game or going someplace new. What action have you not taken because you were uncomfortable about doing it? You can accomplish so much if you try.

It is true—you may not perform an action perfectly at first. This may cause you to give up. This can affect your belief in yourself not only in this instance but also in other circumstances. You may not even attempt a new activity, or you might give up too quickly even though you would be successful if you continued.

Take action! Keep trying. It takes practice to become skillful; we all stumble in the learning process. If you never make mistakes, that means you never try to do anything. Making mistakes is far better than doing nothing at all. What seems difficult to you now may turn out to be enjoyable. Allow yourself to try!

Face each new activity first in the safety of your own thoughts. If you begin to feel any negative emotions, let them go. Allow yourself to think constructive thoughts. Imagine taking this new action. Join with the creative energy of the Universe. Picture your full ability pouring forth. Vividly imagine and feel yourself taking the correct actions and enjoying the situation. When you can clearly see yourself taking action in your mind successfully and joyously, you can actually do it.

Concentrate on your enjoyment and the free expression of your inner Self. Don't force movements; let them flow. Allow your body to relax and let your mind become alert and focused. Don't focus on what you do wrong; continue to gently replace doubt with confidence. With visualization and actual physical practice, these actions become natural to you. You will perform with ease and delight.

Being totally centered on winning can take the joy out of life. It is not necessary to be perfect and successful in every situation to be a winner. How you deal with a situation determines whether or not you are a true winner.

Honesty, courage, and belief in yourself are important. Enjoying the process matters as much as if not more than winning. You are a winner if you take action and do the best you can do. This is a forgiving and loving Universe. Keep having fun and keep trying. Take action and experience the joy that you create!

Quiet Reflection

Sit or lie down with your spine straight. Yawn and s t r e t c h. Close your eyes. Breathe deeply, relax, and let all your muscles go limp. Feel a stream of Light-filled Energy beaming down from the cosmos'and flowing up from the earth. Let this Light flow harmoniously through your body, mind, and spirit, and radiate from every part of your being. Keep breathing deeply and slowly while you go to a quiet place inside yourself. Count back from 10 to 1, relaxing more with each deep breath. Visualize the following:

You are once more on the grounds of your Light-filled crystal palace. Experience the love and energy that pour out to you. Everything you want to accomplish is real for you here. This is your perfect reality, your sanctuary.

The wisdom and creative Energy of the Universe flow through you. Decide if you want to allow the winner inside you to come forward. If you do, see yourself taking the perfect actions toward your goal. Allow your full ability to come forth. In your mind's eye, picture yourself performing better than you ever have before. Feel the energy flow through you. You are one with all of nature; you are one with whatever you need to help you perform. You are a perfect expression of the Universe. You are totally relaxed, confident, and natural. You perform easily and effortlessly, experiencing each moment as if it is the only moment. There is no past, no future—only the now; you experience it to the fullest measure possible. Visualize again and again your perfect performance. Whenever you need to perform at your highest level, you will remember to experience it first in your mind's eye. Your perfect performance will become a reality for you.

Enjoy this feeling of peace for as long as you wish. When you are ready, take a deep breath and begin to move your hands and feet. Stretch and open your eyes.

Message From Within

Contact with your inner wisdom and creativity will bring you enthusiasm and deep confidence. Think about an activity that lies before you and ask your inner Self to help you find the correct actions. Note any feelings, ideas, or images that come to you.

Take Action

Write down what you will accomplish today.

Write down what you will accomplish this week.

Write down what you will accomplish this month.

Write down what you will accomplish this year.

Write down what you will accomplish in the next five years.

Write down what you will accomplish in the next 25 years.

Write down what you will accomplish in your lifetime.

Describe the life you desire to live during your retirement years. What will you do now to prepare for this lifestyle?

Write down the steps you will take to accomplish your goals. Make each step small enough so that you know you can do it, and determine a date to take each step. You can do what you believe you can. Keep trying—be the winner you are!

Burning Desire

I have a burning desire
to perform at my highest level.

Affirmations

I allow the Power of the Universe
to flow through me.
I am filled with creative energy.
I am confident in my ability.
I vividly see myself performing at my best.
I think clearly and act quickly.
Success and fulfillment are mine.

My Personal Affirmations

10

Resolve All Challenges

E.J. Rogers

Creativity can solve almost any problem. The creative act, the defeat of habit by originality, overcomes everything.

—George Lois

Resolve All Challenges

You attract the problems you encounter for the opportunity to learn, grow, and change. With problems comes excitement! Think of problems in this manner and face them with gratitude—turn them into challenges. You can do what you believe you can do. Each time you face a problem with a belief in your ability, determination, and an intense desire for resolution, success becomes easier to achieve.

Write down exactly what the problem is. Contact your creative Self for guidance and solutions and write down the positive steps and actions that feel right to you. Discovering the correct actions will bring a feeling of inner harmony and peace. Describe these steps in great detail and set a date when each action will be completed.

You create what you see in your imagination and that which you have a burning desire to achieve. Frequently visualize these steps being taken easily and successfully.

When you decide what can be done, your difficulty does not seem so overwhelming. With a written plan of action comes inner power. You feel positive and alive. Join with the creative energy of the Universe and take action! Allow yourself to feel the joy of taking this positive action and moving forward one step at a time. If your first plan is unsuccessful, make changes to allow it to work—never give up. Soon your challenge will be resolved. You can direct your life. Always trust yourself; you have the power and the creativity to bring balance and success into your life.

Quiet Reflection

Sit or lie down with your spine straight. Yawn and s t r e t c h. Close your eyes. Breathe deeply, relax, and let all your muscles go limp. Feel a stream of Light-filled Energy beaming down from the cosmos and flowing up from the earth. Let this Light flow harmoniously through your body, mind, and spirit, and radiate from every part of your being. Keep breathing deeply and slowly while you go to a quiet place inside yourself. Count back from 10 to 1, relaxing more with each deep breath. Visualize the following:

Now you will discover a new area of your crystal palace. It holds all your experiences, present and future. Find the door behind which a challenge—a new opportunity for growth—is unfolding. From your deepest Self, feel the confidence inside you begin to grow. Walk into this new situation and live it now!

Say, "Divine wisdom and energy flow through me. I am an open channel for perfect guidance and protection. I open my heart and perfect concentration, quickness, and ability are mine. I am totally relaxed and completely confident."

See yourself taking action to solve your challenge. Picture each action being taken with confidence; see yourself doing each thing easily. Feel yourself smiling. Clearly picture receiving the results you want. Picture every detail—really give the scene life! Feel proud and experience the joy of your success. You can easily handle all of your challenges. When necessary, you will take action with confidence. The power and strength that you experience here will give you the ability to relax and take action with joy.

Enjoy this feeling of peace for as long as you wish. When you are ready, take a deep breath and begin to move your hands and feet. Stretch and open your eyes.

Message From Within

When you face a challenge, don't force actions. Go forward with an inner knowing that now is the time and these are the steps to take. In quiet solitude ask your higher Self to help you develop a solution to a challenge that is before you. Write down any images or thoughts that come to you.

Take Action

List a problem/challenge that you wish to resolve.

What do you want the outcome to be?

Contact your inner knowing for the correct steps to take. List every possible solution. Brainstorm. "Sleep on it" if you don't feel good about the actions to be taken. Let your mind play with it. You may be delighted with the creative solutions that surface.

Decide which steps are the best, then write a detailed plan of action for each step you will take. Beside each step, indicate a date when each step will be taken. Visualize completing each step successfully.

Take the first step of action. Keep trying even if you encounter difficulties, disappointments, and criticism. Keep visualizing your desire until it manifests in your life. Your challenge is very close to being resolved!

Burning Desire

I have a burning desire to deal with
all the challenges in my life.

Affirmations

I see challenges as opportunities
to learn, grow, and change.
I listen to my inner voice
for guidance.
Inspiration pours to me.
My actions come effortlessly.
Divine power and wisdom
flow through me and make me strong.
Doors of opportunity fly open
and achievement floods in.

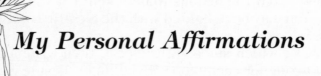

My Personal Affirmations

11

Deal with Difficult People

A loving person lives in a loving world. A hostile person lives in a hostile world: everyone you meet is your mirror.

—Ken Keyes, Jr.

Deal with Difficult People

People who cause a strong emotional reaction in you are extremely important; they bring you tremendous opportunities for growth. You attract people into your life who will help you fulfill your life's plan. They bring lessons to you that you desire to learn.

See opportunities for your growth when dealing with the abrasive actions of others—they are not harming* you as you may think they would like. When you encounter a difficult person, smile to yourself; he or she is helping you grow extremely quickly. Instead of cursing the person, thank him or her. Through people like this you will learn to direct your emotions and grow in strength.

Emotional pain sometimes comes with the lessons of life. How can you grow if everyone is pleasant and loving toward you? How can you learn to feel compassion for others if you do not experience distress? How will you develop the ability to direct your emotions? How can you experience joy without knowing pain?

Everyone does not have to like you for you to respect and love yourself. Your existence doesn't have to be free from conflict for you to lead a joyous life.

For the most part, you determine the way people treat you. If you love and respect yourself, others will treat you with respect. If you think critically of yourself, others will be critical of you. If you have no confidence in yourself, others will have no confidence in you. If you let go of your own destructive thoughts concerning yourself, that change will be reflected in the way you are treated.

People reveal what you like and dislike in yourself. The good you see in others is the good you know in yourself, and the imperfections you see in others may reflect a trait of your own. Take a look at the words and actions of others that irritate you. Do they remind you of your own shortcomings or feelings about yourself? Or perhaps the other person has something you wish you had: power? confidence? security?

---

*If physical or intense emotional pain occurs, remove yourself from this person at once and seek help. This chapter does not refer to actions that put you in great fear or danger.

Search for the root of the conflict. People mirror your feelings about yourself back to you. Does this person intensify feelings you already have regarding yourself? Examine your emotions and determine how you can resolve these feelings. Perhaps then some of the tension between the two of you will also dissolve.

You may think about this person and become upset even when he or she is not around. When you find your thoughts on this person, allow those destructive thoughts to go. Old habits are hard to break, but they can be broken!

You control how you react to the world around you. Some people will treat you poorly. You give up your power if you let someone else's bad mood, sharp tongue, or offensive actions affect you. Do you want to allow another to control your feelings, or do you want to keep responsibility for your emotions and remain calm and unaffected by this person? It is your choice.

Remain detached. Take slow, full breaths and relax. Say to yourself, "I remain unaffected by this negativity. I am divinely guided and protected. I go inside myself and experience deep harmony with the Universe. Positive energy surrounds me and keeps me from harm, and I send positive energy to this person's higher Self for his or her growth and understanding. I am indeed a strong and powerful person. I am now free to continue my day in peace and loving energy."

Have the courage to give difficult people a second chance. Perhaps they had a bad day. Perhaps they have deep-seated emotional problems; maybe someone has hurt them and they have not dealt with it well. Perhaps they have built false personalities to protect themselves. They may be blind to others' feelings because they are working so hard to guard their own. It is possible you are imagining their thoughts and feelings. Perhaps instead of feeling "better" than you, they may feel intimidated by you. You cannot read people's minds. You cannot think clearly if you are in a defensive or fearful state.

Don't try to conquer, control, or even change this person. You teach by example; be a good one. A smile and positive energy may help ease a tense situation. Act with dignity, honor, and confidence. Keep your thoughts pleasant and a smile in your heart.

Try to focus on the person with whom you are interacting. What is he or she saying or feeling; what is his or her body language saying? Try to get involved with truly listening and caring about what the person has to say. Take your focus off yourself. Don't worry about how you look, what the other person will think of you, what you will say next, etc. To make people like you, treat them like you wish to be treated—give them your full attention and respect. Smile and bring a little joy into their day. Be honest in a constructive, productive manner.

There will always be people with whom you have conflict. Don't run away from these people or you will continue to run into them. When you conquer your feelings in dealing with a difficult person, you will be able to face more troublesome situations in the future. Learn to remain untouched by others' destructive behavior and negative energy. Allow yourself to stay in control. You have taken a giant leap toward creating joy in your life.

Quiet Reflection

Sit or lie down with your spine straight. Yawn and s t r e t c h. Close your eyes. Breathe deeply, relax, and let all your muscles go limp. Feel a stream of Light-filled Energy beaming down from the cosmos and flowing up from the earth. Let this Light flow harmoniously through your body, mind, and spirit, and radiate from every part of your being. Keep breathing deeply and slowly while you go to a quiet place inside yourself. Count back from 10 to 1, relaxing more with each deep breath. Visualize the following:

Invite the person with whom you wish to develop a better relationship to join you (in your mind's eye!). Go to an area where you feel totally safe and protected. This can be on your crystal palace grounds or any other place you choose. You may wish to share the joy you have found in your crystal palace, or you may not wish for the other person to enter. It is your choice.

Allow yourself to see beyond the person's human ego and physical body and discover his or her natural, higher Self. Picture this higher Self as a glowing, golden body of Light. This is the light-being you will be dealing with now. Affirm your trust in the wisdom and goodness of his or her higher Self, and allow the other person to experience the love and harmony of the golden light of your higher Self. Affirm that he or she can trust you completely in this pure environment.

Explain that you are not a threat, and you want to peacefully coexist with him or her. You want to treat the other person with respect, and you wish the same treatment in return.

The past is gone; imagine both of you letting it go. Picture the golden Light of your higher Selves increasing. The pain you have experienced in the past and the uneasy feelings you have had toward each other can be seen as dull,

dark spots in your light. Imagine that the dark areas begin to lift and pull away from you; feel a weight being lifted as the darkness gently leaves you both.

See a magnificent sphere of white Light-energy come toward you. Feel the majesty and power of this energy. This glorious white Light fills you and your new friend with tremendous joy and freedom. All is calm. The Light-energy draws the pain from you. You sense arms reaching out for your pain, cradling it, comforting it, and absorbing it. All darkness and pain have totally dissolved from you both; only peace and understanding remain. You are free.

The white Light continues to intensify. Gently you both are surrounded by this extraordinary energy until total peace and harmony fill you. When you leave this protected spot you will take this protecting shield of energy with you.

You have shared your higher Selves with each other. In the future, focus on this highest part of this person and send him or her renewed energy. You are always surrounded with healing, protecting Light. Go in peace.

Enjoy this feeling of peace for as long as you wish. When you are ready, take a deep breath and begin to move your hands and feet. Stretch and open your eyes.

Message From Within

Relax and let all your muscles go limp. Breathe deeply and slowly. Invite the person with whom you have had difficulty in the past to join you in your mind once more. With innocent purity, allow your higher Selves to speak to one another. Ask questions of this person's highest wisdom regarding your relationship. Write down whatever comes to mind.

Take Action

Describe the person with whom you have difficulty. List all his or her traits and actions that upset you.

What would you really like to say to this person? Write all your feelings and thoughts down in a letter to this person (do not mail this letter; this is only to allow all your feelings to surface in order to deal with them).

Select the action or trait that most often triggers a negative response in you. How does this action or trait make you feel?

Why does this bring out so much emotion in you?

How do you deal with your feelings when you are around this person?

What are the most constructive ways you can deal with this person?

How do you deal with your feelings when you are away from
this person?

How can you deal with these feelings in a more constructive
way?

List all the good qualities this person possesses that you
respect.

Say with sincere emotion, "(Name), I desire to release all the negativity I have toward you. This is a new beginning. I break all bonds of negativity. I surround myself with healing energy, and I send you energy for your highest good. Be happy. I am free."

You are in charge of your life. Describe the positive actions, feelings, and thoughts you will now have in the presence of this person. Visualize your new relationship.

Burning Desire

I have a burning desire to direct my emotions
and remain confident and in harmony
when dealing with (name).

Affirmations

I surround myself with the protection of
powerful loving energy.
I easily direct my emotions.
I choose to be calm, confident, and in harmony
with the world around me.
(Name), you have my
permission to grow at your own pace;
to be who you choose to be.
All negativity melts into nothingness.
I send you energy for your highest good;
may peace fill you and comfort you.

My Personal Affirmations

12

Forgive Others

Since nothing we intend is ever faultless, and nothing we attempt ever without error, and nothing we achieve without some measure of finitude and fallibility, we are saved by forgiveness.

—David Augsburger

Forgive Others

Sometimes you respond with pain to others' words or actions toward you. You might experience feelings of worthlessness, bitterness, anger, the desire to get even, resentment, or even hatred. These emotions drain your energy and can make you sick. You cannot control another's words or actions; you can only control your actions and your reaction to them.

If you are in physical danger or suffering extreme mental abuse, take immediate action to remove yourself from harm. Get outside help. It is not acceptable at any time to abuse or to put up with abuse. When you are safe from destructive behavior, then you can focus on becoming free of emotional pain.

Look deep inside yourself. Ask why you had this experience. What do you need to understand about this situation? You may find you are not receiving the good you deserve. This may frustrate or confuse you and could suggest changes which you may fear to make.

Examine the sensitive areas this experience touches. In your adult life, the negative words and actions of others mirror your own deep feelings (be they true ones or illusions). If others' words did not reflect your own feelings, you would be indifferent to them.

You deserve your own love and the respect of others. Change your beliefs about yourself in a positive way and the people around you will treat you in a more positive manner. Picture the supportive treatment you desire and clearly imagine delightful new relationships.

Be strong and rise above the negative actions of others. You cannot change their thoughts or actions, but you can direct your own. When someone makes a mistake or does something that normally would upset you, stay calm. Why allow others to control your emotions? Learn to remain untouched by his or her negativity. Smile and send the person energy for his or her highest growth and understanding. Surround yourself with a shield of protecting Light, and see all negativity bounce off this shield and flow away from you.

Everyone is responsible for his or her actions and follows the path of his or her own choosing. Everyone is on a different level of understanding and compassion for others. Everyone makes mistakes. Learn not to judge others. Without allowing harm to come to yourself, accept others with their fear, ignorance, and imperfections. Each time you feel patience and compassion, you turn on your power.

People learn from their parents and society. Perhaps the negativity they give is the negativity they received; they may have been told the very same words or treated in the same manner in the past. Feel compassion for the pain they must have endured to act this way now. Remember they once were innocent, loving children who grew into what they are today.

If people in the past have hurt you, forgive them or they will continue to hurt you. You do not need to approve of them to forgive them; you do not even need to like them. Just understand that they are human and make mistakes. Let go of the desire to prove you are right or the need to get even. Release your anger, bitterness, and emotional ties with those who have hurt you.

Forgiveness does not mean that you accept cruel behavior, overlook others' actions, or let them continue to hurt you. It does not mean that you pretend an incident did not happen or that you believe their actions were acceptable.

Forgiveness means you are free. It means you acknowledge human imperfection and can create harmony and love in spite of it. Humans are sometimes hidden from their true perfection in this existence. Forgiveness reopens the door to the Light.

In learning to forgive others, you learn to forgive yourself. You may not know how to forgive. Request help from the Higher Power to be able to forgive, and ask that love and compassion flow through you and guide you.

In your heart, appeal to the highest part of the one who hurt you. Focus on the small, innocent child he or she was at birth. Focus on the highest part of the person that is waiting to be expressed.

Try, for your own peace, to feel love for the higher Self that yearns to be free deep within the person. Wish for the person a higher understanding of what he or she needs to know regarding this situation. Send Light-filled energy for his or her highest growth and wisdom. Send love to the empty part that needs love so urgently. Forgive him or her for your own good.

Are you willing to forgive? If you are, you have forgiven, and you are free.

You are just as you should be at this moment: you are a child of the Universe. Allow yourself to be at peace again. Be healed. You are, indeed, a powerful and loving person. Perfect harmony and wisdom flow within you, and the love of the Universe is always with you.

Quiet Reflection

Sit or lie down with your spine straight. Yawn and s t r e t c h. Close your eyes. Breathe deeply, relax, and let all your muscles go limp. Feel a stream of Light-filled Energy beaming down from the cosmos and flowing up from the earth. Let this Light flow harmoniously through your body, mind, and spirit, and radiate from every part of your being. Keep breathing deeply and slowly while you go to a quiet place inside yourself. Count back from 10 to 1, relaxing more with each deep breath. Visualize the following:

Go once more up the mountain path to your crystal palace; feel your energy and power build as you come closer. Imagine a Light-filled garden outside the palace. Fill the garden with plants, flowers, trees, fountains and streams, or whatever brings you peace and delight.

Picture a cylindrical shield of iridescent Light swirling around you, boring deep into the earth. The cylinder is open to the soothing, radiant energy that flows down from the cosmos and up from the earth. You are divinely protected. Bring to mind the person you want most to forgive. Send thoughts of peace to this person's higher Self and ask Divine Wisdom to guide him or her to a higher awareness and a fuller life. Feel deep within your heart an outpouring of love for the person's perfect inner beauty. Forgive him or her for negativity and human imperfections. See the cloud of pain and confusion lift from you both. See it being sucked into the swirling cylinder of light and taken down—down into the ground where it changes into nourishment for the earth. Pour out love and goodwill to this person. You will remain protected from negativity and pain. You are powerful and free.

Enjoy this feeling of peace for as long as you wish. When you are ready, take a deep breath and begin to move your hands and feet. Stretch and open your eyes.

Message From Within

Bring to mind the person you most need to forgive. Remember his or her words and actions that brought you pain. Look deep inside yourself for an understanding of what this situation can teach you. Write down everything that comes to you.

Take Action

Who is the person you most need to forgive? Write a letter to the person who was involved. (Do not mail this letter. This is not to hurt someone, it is to acknowledge your pain in order to let it go.) Describe his or her words and actions. Describe in detail your emotions at the time and the emotions that you now have when you recall this. Write everything you wish to say to this person.

Why do you think the person you most need to forgive did what he or she did?

Write down how you would like to feel now.

You are in charge now. Do you want to be free of pain that developed so long ago? You do not need to accept the actions of the other person, just be willing to forgive his or her human imperfections. What will you do to forgive and heal yourself?

Say, "I forgive you, (name). I let go of the pain from my body, mind, and spirit. I release you and I send you peace. I fill myself with loving, healing Light. I am free."

Burning Desire

I have a burning desire to
forgive all who have hurt me.

Affirmations

Loving energy surrounds me and protects me.
Walls of negativity crumble around me.
I let go of resentment and hate.
All who have hurt me are forgiven.
I send them understanding and goodwill.
I fill myself with
jubilant love and healing peace.

My Personal Affirmations

13

Accept Others As They Are

If a man does not keep pace with his companions, perhaps it is because he hears a different drummer. Let him step to the music which he hears, however measured or far away.

—Henry David Thoreau

Accept Others As They Are

You are so much more than the body you see! In your most quiet moments you have caught glimpses of your true Self and have felt the strength and beauty of your eternal spirit.

There is a divine plan for your life. Each person developed their own plan with the Higher Power of the Universe before they came into this life. Each has lessons to learn and knowledge to discover; emotions to understand and direct. Each person has the free will to decide what he or she now chooses to do in this life.

You may be on different awareness levels but no one person is better than another. You are free to find your own truth and grow at your own pace.

Each person in this world is different from every other. It is everyone's right to look, think, and feel the way that is best for him or her. Each person is responsible for his or her own life and must follow his or her own inner guidance.

The variety in life makes living exciting. You take delight in each color of the rainbow; each color has its place and is perfect in its existence. So it is with each color of skin; with each set of beliefs; with each set of feelings and desires. Treasure the right to be an individual! You will be happier for it, and the Universe will be happier, too.

You may have been taught that only one color was the right color; that only one religion was the right religion. You may have been taught much that keeps you from being open and accepting toward others. You control your thoughts now. You decide what is right and wrong. Allow yourself to re-examine old beliefs and decide for yourself what you feel in your heart.

Let go of the expectation that people should be just like you, and allow others the freedom to learn and grow. Let them follow their inner guidance; allow them to be their true, honest selves. If they falter, do not judge them. Everyone makes mistakes. Recognize their imperfections and choose your response. You may choose to move on, but do not try to change or control them.

Share your thoughts, but do not try to force others to think as you do. Replace negative feelings toward them with compassion. Send them positive, loving energy to use for their highest good.

Accept others, with their goodness and imperfections, as you desire to be accepted. Do not try to change or control them. Everyone is created and loved by the same Power. Accept these expressions of the Universe exactly as they are.

Quiet Reflection

Sit or lie down with your spine straight. Yawn and s t r e t c h. Close your eyes. Breathe deeply, relax, and let all your muscles go limp. Feel a stream of Light-filled Energy beaming down from the cosmos and flowing up from the earth. Let this Light flow harmoniously through your body, mind, and spirit, and radiate from every part of your being. Keep breathing deeply and slowly while you go to a quiet place inside yourself. Count back from 10 to 1, relaxing more with each deep breath. Visualize the following:

You are lying against an oak tree in a sunny meadow near your crystal palace. You are filled with deep peace and inner joy. The energy and love of your higher Self flows through you. You are open to ideas from the truest part of yourself. A light, warm rain begins to fall. Through an opening in the clouds a brilliant ray of sunlight is beaming down. Before your eyes a magnificent rainbow appears. Red, orange, yellow, green, blue, and violet stretch out before you. Up and up you float until you take your place in this spectrum of light. Experience the glory of each color existing in unity; each color is an equal and vital part of the rainbow's totality. Feel the harmony of this perfect blending.

Open your heart and take delight in each color of the rainbow. Each color originates from the same Light. So it is with different colors of skin, with different beliefs, and with different desires. Everyone is created and loved by the same Power; everyone is part of the Whole. We all are one. Accept these perfect expressions of the Universe just the way they are.

Enjoy this feeling of peace for as long as you wish. When you are ready, take a deep breath and begin to move your hands and feet. Stretch and open your eyes.

Message From Within

Trust in your own perfect inner wisdom with an open heart and mind. Relax. Just let go. Who do you most need to learn to accept? Ask the highest part of yourself to uncover that which you need to know about accepting other people. Write down anything and everything that comes to mind.

Take Action

Write down why someone who is different from you makes you feel uncomfortable. List how these differences might benefit the world.

Why do you think this person makes you uncomfortable?

What do you think you need to learn from this person?

Write down all the ways you can imagine that this person is similar to you.

Describe the world if all people began to view others with understanding, compassion, and love.

Burning Desire

I have a burning desire to
accept others as they are.

Affirmations

We are all loved by the same Power.
We are all a part of the Whole.
I feel compassion for others
even if they falter.
I recognize each person's
inner love and wisdom.
Everyone is exactly as he or she
should be at this moment.
I accept each person as a perfect
expression of the Universe.

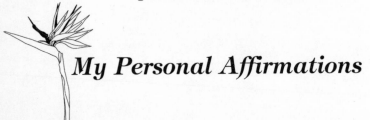

My Personal Affirmations

14

Let Go of the Past

... life goes not backward nor tarries with yesterday.
—Kahlil Gibran

Let Go of the Past

The past is gone and cannot be changed. Only the way you feel about it can be changed. If you let the past haunt you, joy cannot be yours. Bring your thoughts under control and back to this moment in time; this moment is where your power is.

You control your thoughts and how you react to them. Think thoughts that make you one with the Universe instead of thoughts that make you fearful and alone.

Thinking of a painful past experience is living it again. You are only hurting yourself. You may be giving the past more energy than you give the present moment. Does it make you feel better? Does it make it change? Does reliving a painful experience bring any good to you? No? Then let it go! It is never too late to change old beliefs and teachings. Let go of a painful memory if it harms you in the present moment, and rediscover yourself and the world.

In the past you may have hurt someone. Is this person still affected by your actions? Does he or she remember your actions? If you think he or she does, take action to resolve these old feelings. It is never too late. In order to let go of the past, take responsibility for your actions. If you have hurt someone, take action to right the wrong. If it is not possible to do this physically, then do it with your thoughts. Ask forgiveness and send the other person loving energy for his or her highest good. Forgive yourself.

As a child you may have felt unloved, not quite good enough, or not smart enough. You may have learned to dislike yourself. You cannot let go of the past if you continue to feel this negativity about yourself. Will you continue to hurt yourself the way you feel others have?

You are in control now. Only you can break this cycle of pain. Will you allow yourself to support the little child that waits inside you? Introduce yourself to the innocent little child you once were. This tender being has been waiting to be comforted for a long time; waiting to be loved and accepted just the way he or she is. Can you do it?

Be gentle with yourself. Be free of the past. Start fresh and teach the child inside you how to love! Learn to love yourself again.

You are who you think you are. Begin now to see the good in that special child inside you. You are a perfect creation of wisdom and love. Discover the truth of who you are!

If you feel bitterness, anger, jealousy, self-doubt, or self-hatred, let it go. Let go of any fear or destructive feelings you now have. If someone from whom you wanted love hurt you, decide now if you want to continue to feel the pain. If you choose to move on, forgive the person or he or she will continue to hurt you. To forgive, you do not need to feel that the other person was right in acting as he or she did. Wish for the other person a higher understanding of whatever it is he or she needs to know. Forgive the other person and send him or her peace.

When you wish to let go of hate and be filled with loving energy instead, you can do it. When you desire peace of mind more than you wish to get even, you can do it. When you desire to feel strong and confident more than you wish to feel sorry for yourself, you can do it. When you want to live each moment of your life in joy more than you wish to change the past, you can do it!

To grow you must let go of the past. You are constantly changing. You can direct this change by directing your thoughts. Take control and be free of the past! Put your trust in a loving, forgiving Universe.

Quiet Reflection

Sit or lie down with your spine straight. Yawn and s t r e t c h. Close your eyes. Breathe deeply, relax, and let all your muscles go limp. Feel a stream of Light-filled Energy beaming down from the cosmos and flowing up from the earth. Let this Light flow harmoniously through your body, mind, and spirit, and radiate from every part of your being. Keep breathing deeply and slowly while you go to a quiet place inside yourself. Count back from 10 to 1, relaxing more with each deep breath. Visualize the following:

You are lying in a field of soft clover near your crystal palace. Relax, sink down onto the ground, and feel the strength of the earth flow into your body. Reach out to connect with the planet beneath you. Send tiny roots into the nourishing soil. Your connection with the energy of the earth grows; your roots go deeper and grow stronger. Feel how solid and secure you are! Now you can bury the past. Let it leave your mind, body, and spirit. All your pain will transform into nourishment for the earth. Let your pain flow out into the ground. Every drop of pain from your past moves down the intricate root system, deeper and deeper into the earth. You can see it for what it is as it moves away from you. Allow it to be your teacher. Become aware of why you experienced it, and discover what you can learn from having endured this pain. Become stronger and more compassionate toward others because of it. Be thankful to be able to make the best of a bad situation. As the pain from your past flows away it is broken up and transformed. Further and further it flows into the forgiving planet, changing into nourishing energy. Say goodbye to your pain as it dissolves, never to be part of your experience again. You are free!

Enjoy this feeling of peace for as long as you wish. When you are ready, take a deep breath and begin to move your hands and feet. Stretch and open your eyes.

Message From Within

Only by acknowledging your pain from the past can you allow it to leave you. All you need to know is buried deep inside you. Allow images from the past that hurt you to rise to the surface and write down in detail all the emotions these memories bring. Let your deepest understanding of what these emotions can teach you flow to you.

Take Action

What in your past brings you the most pain?

Your feelings are valid. In order to understand your feelings, describe them.

What purpose does continuing to feel pain from this situation serve?

What can you do to allow this pain to leave you so that it does not continue to hurt you?

Try to make a bad situation work for you. Find something positive about having experienced it. How can you grow from this situation? What has it taught you? How has it made you stronger?

Completely rewrite this situation. Instead of the pain that you experienced, describe the loving, respectful treatment you were entitled to receive.

Burning Desire

I have a burning desire to
let go of the past
and enjoy the present moment.

Affirmations

I forgive all who have hurt me; they are free.
I order negativity to leave every part of me.
The past is gone; I let it go.
This moment brings a new beginning;
a fresh start.
I am thankful to be a part
of a loving Universe.
Soothing Light and love
flow through me.

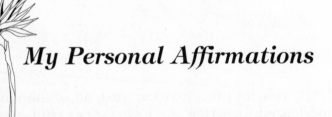

My Personal Affirmations

15

Release Guilt

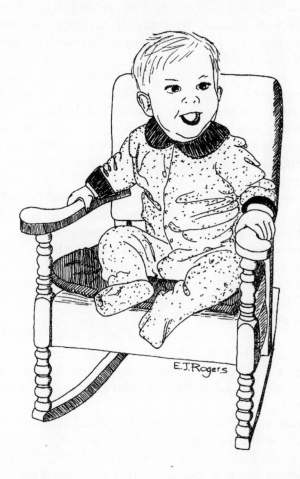

Compassion for myself is the most powerful healer of them all.

—Theodore Isaac Rubin

Release Guilt

Sometimes you might bring pain to another. Sometimes you might do, or just desire to do, something that you consider "wrong." This may cause you guilt or self-hatred. Do not judge yourself; there is no right or wrong regarding your actions. Through actions that result in pain, you discover what actions not to take in the future. Through actions that result in joy, you find your true path.

Society, parents, religions, and other groups make rules to control you for the higher good. Some are valid and necessary rules, and some are not. Now is the time to find your own truth. Only you have the knowledge of what is good for you and what is not good for you. Develop your own values that preserve the well-being and respect of all. Follow your own inner guidance.

Guilt destroys with its self-punishment and pain. Do not fill yourself with disgust regarding your actions, but with deep compassion. Do not waste your energy on guilt. Take steps to turn your negative emotions into positive ones. Discover where your guilt originated and decide what you need to do to act responsibly. Feel an obligation for your actions, not guilt. Make amends, learn from your mistakes, and change your actions in the future.

Let go of misunderstanding and guilt. Talk to the person you feel you have hurt and explain your actions. Tell the person you regret this conflict. Hopefully, he or she will release you. You are worthy of a second chance; you are worthy of being forgiven.

If you cannot speak to this person, send him or her healing thoughts. Imagine saying you are sorry if you brought him or her pain. Fill the person with the Light of peace and love and picture him or her healed. Love and goodwill pulsate through both of you. You are released! Forgive yourself and let the pain be gone.

If your remorse is not valid, discover why you are punishing yourself. Have you learned to feel this way from teachings from your past? You are responsible for the way you feel now. Reexamine your beliefs and decide what is for your highest good. Get rid of feelings of guilt that keep you from enjoying this moment and being the best you can be.

Release the past. Let go of shame and regret through new awareness and positive action. Follow your own inner guidance. Bring harm to no one, including yourself. Acknowledge the perfection and goodness within you; you are growing and there is perfection in this growth. Live life fully, as you desire. Follow your heart—it lights the way to the joy and freedom you seek.

Quiet Reflection

Sit or lie down with your spine straight. Yawn and s t r e t c h. Close your eyes. Breathe deeply, relax, and let all your muscles go limp. Feel a stream of Light-filled Energy beaming down from the cosmos and flowing up from the earth. Let this Light flow harmoniously through your body, mind, and spirit, and radiate from every part of your being. Keep breathing deeply and slowly while you go to a quiet place inside yourself. Count back from 10 to 1, relaxing more with each deep breath. Visualize the following:

Go once more to your crystal palace. Create a special place for yourself here. Harmonize with the love and acceptance that wait for you deep inside your own heart.

    Light a candle and gaze into the flickering golden fire. Say to yourself, "I have a burning desire to release all guilt. From this moment forward I will bring harm to no one. I am a person of high character and integrity and I take full responsibility for my actions. I act with the well-being of myself and others in mind. I search deep inside myself for truth and I follow my sound inner guidance. I forgive myself! I will learn to love and accept myself completely, starting now. I am free."

    The cleansing flame burns away everything from the past that has caused you pain. Unfair and invalid restrictions and beliefs burn away; guilt and negativity flame into nothingness. The gentle flicker of dancing light continues to burn away your feelings of guilt, shame, and remorse. You are cleansed from pain and all negative emotions. The tongue of fire becomes a brilliant display of the wisdom and purity of your soul.

Enjoy this feeling of peace for as long as you wish. When you are ready, take a deep breath and begin to move your hands and feet. Stretch and open your eyes.

Message From Within

In quiet solitude think of what brings you feelings of guilt. Trust your highest knowing to reveal to you what you need to know about this guilt. Write down anything and everything that comes to you.

Take Action

List your actions, thoughts, or desires that now bring you feelings of guilt.

Why do you feel these actions/thoughts/desires are wrong? Are any of the reasons legitimate?

What actions will you take to eliminate your need for this guilt?

When will you take these steps?

Burning Desire

I have a burning desire to release
all guilt and pain from my heart.

Affirmations

This moment is a new beginning.
I am like a child
filled with innocence and joy.
I find the Universe is forgiving.
I use my energy for love and joy,
not guilt and pain.
Light and love flow through me.
I am soothed by the divine arms
of the Universe.

My Personal Affirmations

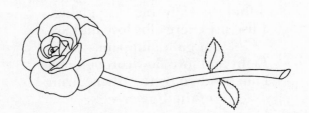

16

Develop Self-Esteem

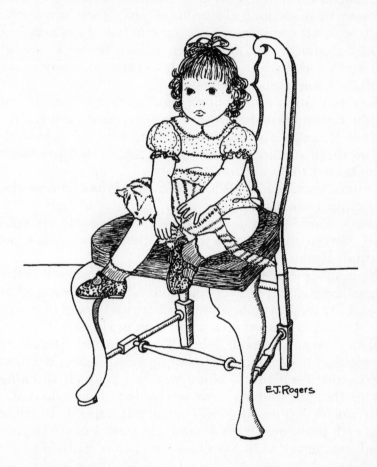

Remember, no one can make you feel inferior without your consent.

—Eleanor Roosevelt

135

Develop Self-Esteem

You determine how you act and therefore how people will react to you. Others are annoyed by your shyness or your inferior feelings. They will not treat you more gently because of a weak, fearful attitude. Many don't want to waste time with someone who does not feel that he or she deserves respect. You attract what you think you deserve in life. If you look and act like a victim you are more likely to be a victim; be afraid of the world and the world will push you around. Learn to act with dignity, and respect belongs to you.

You may think others don't want to talk to you. If you feel this way and remain silent, some people will not realize your true feelings. They may even think you are conceited, that you think you are too good for them, or that you don't want to bother to speak to them.

Others may look confident, but this is not always the case. Others cannot read your mind; don't try to read someone else's mind. You just can't do it! Many people are concerned more with what you think of them than with what they think of you.

Remember that a smile says a thousand words—it is the universal language that everyone understands. It says, "I'm here and I'm glad to be here; you're here and I'm glad you're here." A smile will open up a whole new world to you. Try it!

What you think about yourself is important. Decide to allow yourself to develop self-honor and confidence. Begin to have positive "self talk." When you find yourself thinking thoughts that put yourself down or that say "I can't do that," stop them. Tell yourself good things will happen. Imagine acting with poise and trust in yourself. Say "I can!" Picture yourself taking action in a positive way. Allow yourself to say good things about yourself. Take action with composure and dignity.

Choose the demeanor you wish to portray. Think of a person who has the traits you wish to have, and picture how that person would act in a situation that you often face. Imagine the emotions and thoughts he or she might have. Say and do what you think he or she would say and do. Think of this person as your advisor. When a situation arises and you need a little strength, draw courage from this person who can handle any situation. Let the energy flow. Soon by taking action, you will become stronger. With continued action you will be naturally confident and secure.

With each new situation decide how you want to respond. It will be a challenge for a time. Give yourself love and support, and imagine the positive benefits that will come with your new attitude. Delight in the pleasure your self-esteem will bring. You can direct your thoughts and your actions. Soon you will easily and naturally react to situations with self-confidence and composure. Let your true self emerge and be the whole, complete person you are!

Quiet Reflection

Sit or lie down with your spine straight. Yawn and s t r e t c h. Close your eyes. Breathe deeply, relax, and let all your muscles go limp. Feel a stream of Light-filled Energy beaming down from the cosmos and flowing up from the earth. Let this Light flow harmoniously through your body, mind, and spirit, and radiate from every part of your being. Keep breathing deeply and slowly while you go to a quiet place inside yourself. Count back from 10 to 1, relaxing more with each deep breath. Visualize the following:

Walk up the path to your Light-filled crystal palace. Experience deep within your own heart the love and energy that wait for you here. This is indeed a magical, powerful place. It contains everything you have ever wanted; all the feelings you have ever desired to experience. The self-respect and confidence you want bubble forth inside you here. This crystal palace opens doors to your own enlightenment, your own highest knowing. Here you experience your higher Self. Visualize yourself happy, calm, and confident. Unlock the power inside you! What you visualize in the protected, powerful walls of this Light-filled retreat will create your highest good and your greatest joy. Let the complete and awesome you emerge! Experience yourself as the person you have always wanted to be— become your very best. Experience yourself as a perfect creation of the Universe. Discover your true, natural Self. Find the totality of who you are deep inside your own being. You are a magnificent creation! Accept the confidence and esteem that belong to you.

Enjoy this feeling of peace for as long as you wish. When you are ready, take a deep breath and begin to move your hands and feet. Stretch and open your eyes.

Message From Within

Messages from your higher Self come to you through your thoughts, feelings, and images. Ask for an understanding of how to develop self-esteem. Write down anything that comes to you.

Take Action

How do you feel about yourself?

If you listed any negative feelings, where did these feelings originate?

When you focus on only negative feelings about yourself, you block out other possibilities. Describe the positive way you want to feel about yourself.

What is keeping you from loving yourself and having high self-esteem?

What will allow you to have high self-esteem?

List the positive things that would occur if you developed high self-esteem.

Burning Desire

I have a burning desire to respect
myself as a perfect creation of the Universe.

Affirmations

I am divinely guided and protected.
I request, and Infinite Power responds.
I am a child of the Universe,
a creation of inner wisdom and love.
I am one with all of creation.
Strength and courage flow through me.
Peace and confidence are mine.

My Personal Affirmations

17

Love and Accept Yourself

E.J.Rogers

You are a child of the Universe, no less than the trees and the stars; you have a right to be here. And whether or not it is clear to you, no doubt the Universe is unfolding as it should.

—Max Ehrmann

Love and Accept Yourself

Accept yourself as a creation of beauty; delight in yourself exactly as you are. Love yourself with your goodness and your imperfections. You were meant to have imperfections in this lifetime, yet you long for perfection, for goodness, beauty, and truth. This search is essential for your growth. In this seeking you find your way back to the Light.

Be gentle with yourself. You are creating and growing; your Divine Plan is unfolding in its own perfect way. You came to this earth with extraordinary potential and abilities as well as limitations. Accept yourself as you are! Enjoy the freedom to just be you.

Be kind to yourself when looking at your imperfections. You are just as you should be even with your human shortcomings. Do not hide from them or hide them from yourself, but accept your imperfections tenderly. Treat them as confusion searching for truth. Allow them to reveal the lessons they contain, then learn these lessons and let them go.

Be honest with yourself. To recognize the best in yourself presents the difficult responsibility to live up to it. To acknowledge the worst in yourself is to decide whether or not to accept it and stay the same. To continue to hold false beliefs about yourself is never to realize your full potential.

Trust yourself completely. Search deep inside yourself for the truth of who you are. Let your genuine Self emerge. Be the best you can be! Discover your deepest yearnings, hopes, and dreams. Be free to learn, change, and grow into the full reality of you.

It is necessary to love and accept yourself in order to create a joyous life. You are worthy of love. Instead of trying to make the world love you, love yourself! Only then can you give and receive love fully and create a joyous and fulfilling life.

You may think you are someone you are not. When you were young you may have been taught that you were not good enough. You may have felt unwanted, worthless, or even unloved. You were good enough! That small child was innocent and pure. You were perfect—you *are* perfect! Let go of old thoughts, teachings, and beliefs that are not valid. At this moment, exactly the way you are, you are a perfect creation of the Universe!

Your thoughts create who you are and how you feel about yourself. Do you find yourself focusing on the worst in yourself? If you want to dislike yourself, think terrible thoughts regarding yourself and focus on your shortcomings, past mistakes, and qualities you do not like.

Thinking negatively about yourself does nothing to benefit you. Putting yourself down will not influence others to build you up or convince others that you are wise because you are aware of your shortcomings. Thinking destructive thoughts about yourself doesn't help you change for the better; it is only an excuse to keep you from taking positive action. It keeps you from being your best.

Do you want to feel badly about yourself, or do you want to learn to love yourself? Give up the need to hurt yourself and make yourself feel bad. Let go of self-pity, frustration, self-doubt, and depression. These feelings take away your joy, energy, and ability to act.

Improve the thoughts about yourself and you improve yourself. It takes a burning desire to redirect your thought patterns. Become aware of your thoughts and you will be able to redirect them. If you want to like yourself, think positive thoughts about yourself.

Begin now to stop all destructive thoughts about yourself. Self-destructive thoughts kill your joy and keep you from being your best. Take charge of your thoughts right now and concentrate on who you want to be. Allow yourself to make positive statements about yourself, even if you don't fully believe them yet. Immediately stop allowing yourself to think and make negative comments about yourself. This is a challenge, and only you can do it.

Use your thoughts in ways that will support you. Think thoughts that present yourself as the best person you can be; thoughts that boost your confidence. Think of yourself the way you want to be—you are what you think you are! Allow yourself to feel good and learn to be proud of yourself.

Develop thoughts that encourage positive actions and feelings of self-worth and strength. Focus on how you want to feel. Form a plan of action that will allow you to love and respect yourself. Don't be afraid to allow the natural, genuine you to emerge. Picture yourself confidently taking action to fulfill this plan and accomplishing what you want. Your thoughts are powerful! Use them to support instead of cripple yourself.

Change your negative thoughts about yourself to loving, constructive thoughts. This may be the most difficult and the most rewarding action of your life. Create joy and bring laughter into your life. Learn to love and accept yourself and you will be well on your way to creating a joyous life.

True love and acceptance do not come from outside of you, they come from deep inside yourself. You are, right now, a perfect creation of inner wisdom and beauty. Reach for your own love—bathe in its truth, its purity, and its joy. Love and accept yourself fully. Love and be one with the Light.

Quiet Reflection

Sit or lie down with your spine straight. Yawn and s t r e t c h. Close your eyes. Breathe deeply, relax, and let all your muscles go limp. Feel a stream of Light-filled Energy beaming down from the cosmos and flowing up from the earth. Let this Light flow harmoniously through your body, mind, and spirit, and radiate from every part of your being. Keep breathing deeply and slowly while you go to a quiet place inside yourself. Count back from 10 to 1, relaxing more with each deep breath. Visualize the following:

Feel yourself drawn to the love and peace of your highest Self. Dance and laugh your way up the path to your Light-filled crystal palace. Something wonderful is waiting for you; its energy draws you near and fills you with excitement. As you burst through the welcoming doors you are overwhelmed by a magnificent pink Light that fills you with unconditional love and total acceptance. Feel the Light growing warmer and stronger, filling your heart and flowing through your veins. Feel the tingle of love spreading throughout your body. Feel the strength and the power your love brings you. Say to yourself, "I am exactly as I should be at this moment. My inner wisdom and love surround me. I love and accept myself exactly as I am. I am a perfect expression of inner wisdom and beauty." Allow yourself to say, "I respect myself ... I like myself ... I accept myself ... I love myself ..." over and over until you believe these statements with all your heart. Feel the warm Light caress you gently, lovingly ... experience the joy of your heart. Bathe in its truth and purity. You are, right now, a perfect and loving being.

Enjoy this feeling of peace for as long as you wish. When you are ready, take a deep breath and begin to move your hands and feet. Stretch and open your eyes.

Message From Within

Be gentle when looking at your feelings about yourself; do not hide from them. Accept yourself tenderly. Bring to mind how you were treated as a small child. How were you shown love? You are the adult now that directs your life. You can show the little child inside you all the love that he or she needs and deserves. Embrace this innocent child inside you! Tell the child everything he or she longs to hear. Express all the love you have for the small child inside of you; let the words pour out. Write down all that comes to you.

Take Action

Do you have a burning desire to be happy? Will you develop self-love in order to be happy?

List the negative qualities you think you have.

For each negative quality you listed, decide if it is true or not. If it is false, mark it out. If it is true, decide if you want to change it or accept it. If you want to change it, put a circle around it. Be gentle with yourself. For each quality you choose to change, describe how you want to be.

You have the power to change your thoughts and actions. When you find yourself thinking destructive thoughts, gently let them go. Then, with enthusiasm and energy, think a positive thought about yourself. You can do it!

Burning Desire

I have a burning desire to love
and accept myself exactly as I am.

Affirmations

I am exactly as I should be
at this moment.
I am a perfect creation of inner beauty and love.
I like myself! I like myself! I like myself!
I respect myself! I respect myself!
I respect myself!
I accept myself! I accept myself!
I accept myself!
I love myself! I love myself! I love myself!

My Personal Affirmations

18

Understand Your Emotions

E.J. Rogers

Your pain is the breaking of the shell that encloses your understanding. Even as the stone of the fruit must break, that its heart may stand in the sun, so must you know pain.

—Kahlil Gibran

Understand Your Emotions

A painful emotion is a brilliant teacher and guide. It can be one of the most powerful forces in your life. Pain encourages you to reevaluate your life; it can startle you into directing your life on a truer course. See pain as a guide instead of a block and it will lead you in the direction you truly want to go.

In this life you are here to grow in love and wisdom. Learn all that your emotions have to teach you. Deal with each small trouble in a positive and effective manner. What actions can you take to change a bad situation into a good one? By working through your pain you become strong; by experiencing pain you gain compassion for others in similar situations.

Pain is not a punishment; it does not exist to make your life miserable. Without pain you cannot truly appreciate and experience joy. The amount of pain you feel is often the amount of joy you have felt about the same thing.

You are meant to enjoy life. You deserve to be happy! Yet it is normal to have feelings of sadness, anger, or fear as long as they are not prolonged. Acknowledge and express your true feelings. Always find a constructive way to let all your emotional energy escape. When you learn to direct your emotions in a positive way you become powerful and you will be able to think clearly. Your energy will be used to take positive action. If deep grief or loss comes, you will be better prepared to deal with it.

Discover what your pain has to teach you. Take positive action to enable your pain to go, and allow it to be replaced with healing, loving energy. Joy and comfort wait for you—bring them into your heart and into your life.

Quiet Reflection

Sit or lie down with your spine straight. Yawn and s t r e t c h. Close your eyes. Breathe deeply, relax, and let all your muscles go limp. Feel a stream of Light-filled Energy beaming down from the cosmos and flowing up from the earth. Let this Light flow harmoniously through your body, mind, and spirit, and radiate from every part of your being. Keep breathing deeply and slowly while you go to a quiet place inside yourself. Count back from 10 to 1, relaxing more with each deep breath. Visualize the following:

Picture your emotions as a small, lost child crying in the dark for comfort and love. Carry the child up the mountain to your crystal palace of self-love. Rock the child and hold him or her gently in your arms. Let the child tell you every detail of how he or she feels. Tell the child it is safe to feel these emotions. Let the emotions out. Let the child scream and cry.

Your emotions have wisdom buried deep inside them. Turn on the light and face them. You are strong and wise; you are protected and guided. Do not be afraid of your emotions; they are your teachers. They reveal your innermost thoughts and feelings. Go deep inside and ask what lessons they reveal. Trust your highest inner knowing to help understand and grow from your feelings.

You are a child of the Universe—a perfect creation of inner truth and love. Divine love protects you; divine wisdom guides you. Surround your newfound truth with loving Light.

Enjoy this feeling of peace for as long as you wish. When you are ready, take a deep breath and begin to move your hands and feet. Stretch and open your eyes.

Message From Within

In quiet solitude, acknowledge any painful emotion you may be holding deep inside. This emotion has much to say to you. Allow wisdom to flow from the deepest part of you. Discover the truth your emotion reveals. Write down the thoughts and feelings that emerge; the more you write, the more feelings will come out. Acknowledge all your feelings—don't bury them or run away from them. Only by acknowledging that they are present can you comfort yourself and learn to let them go.

Take Action

What are the five negative emotions you experience repeatedly in your life?

Describe a situation that often brings you one of these negative emotions.

What is this emotion telling you? What do you need to understand? What inside you caused you to feel this emotion?

You cannot control other's actions, but you do control your feelings. What will allow you to let your negative feelings go? What will you do to ensure you will have control over this emotion in the future?

Burning Desire

I have a burning desire to release
all sadness and pain.

Affirmations

From this moment forward,
I let go of the past.
I release all anger, guilt,
resentment, confusion, fear,
criticism, and hatred. I let them go.
From this moment forward, my every
thought is positive and my every word is good.
My future holds the bright promise of joy.
Love overflows. I am at peace.

My Personal Affirmations

19

Be Healthy

The sorrow which has no vent in tears may make other organs weep.

—Henry Maudsley

Be Healthy

The power inside you knows how to repair your body and keep you well. Trust your body's power. Eat fresh, natural foods that keep you fit and strong. Breathe in air deeply and fully. Allow yourself to relax and be peaceful. Get the rest your body needs, and exercise to keep your body supple and energetic. Express your emotions and let go of negativity. Resolve and then let go of painful emotions from the past. Seek outside support if you need it. Bring harm to no one, including yourself. Develop your connection with the Higher Power of the Universe and allow Light-filled energy to flow to you at your request. Love and accept yourself and others. Take care of your body, mind, and spirit so that your body can take care of you.

Listen to your body's messages to you; this will let you know if something is wrong. Illness is a clue that something needs to be changed; it is your body communicating with you in a way that you cannot ignore. Give thanks for your body's miraculous system that teaches you about yourself and your deepest emotions.

Your body is a magnificent instrument. Your body gives you what you give it—what you put in you get out. Accept and love your body, especially in illness and pain. Learn what it can teach you. Look deep inside yourself and discover what your body is telling you. Only then can you be free of the fear and despair of illness and pain.

If you do become ill, search deep inside yourself for the meaning of the illness. Are you being true to yourself in all areas of your life? Do you have emotions trapped inside that cannot show themselves in any other way? Negativity such as bitterness, fear, hatred, and jealousy can make you sick. Let those feelings leave you or they will bring you more pain. Replace these emotions with compassion and love.

Do not feel guilty about a body that is not perfect. Everything is exactly as it should be. Your Divine Plan reaches beyond this life. You played a major role in developing this

Plan. You may have selected this body with certain weaknesses or you may have planned, on a higher level, for an accident to come into your life. There is order in each illness or weakness of the body. Your higher Self is aware of the purpose; a lesson is awaiting discovery.

If you were born with a condition that cannot be changed, embrace it as a part of yourself. Accept it because you love every part of yourself fully. You are enough, just as you are. You are perfect, even with physical disabilities. Fill yourself with a feeling of peace and well-being. You are one with all the Universe, a creation of perfect beauty and love.

There is perfection in each moment of your existence. Look for the underlying lessons that your condition brings you. These circumstances bring an opportunity for growth. Do not hate your body for reflecting back your life to you. Do not despise the lessons your higher Self chooses to explore.

The lessons your illness bring you may not be just learning how to get well or discovering what caused your illness, but learning to accept yourself and your life. Accept and love your body, especially in illness and pain. Develop peace of mind. Learn to accept what life brings you without fear and live life to its fullest measure at every moment, not just when you feel your best or when life is perfect. Enjoy this moment, for in this moment lies eternity.

Illness can teach you compassion for others and help you grow. The growth could be your own or even for someone else in your life. It can draw the people in your life together and teach them powerful lessons about themselves. Illness can let you and others become stronger for having experienced it.

There is a plan for every moment of your life, even if it is not clear to you. This does not mean you can act with recklessness. Free will is always present, and your plan is constantly adjusting from choices you make and your accomplishments. There is organization and order to each moment even though the mind cannot understand its magnificent depth.

Seemingly painful experiences can bring unexpected opportunities. The sooner you accept your situation as if you had chosen it, the sooner you can start to progress. When you take responsibility for your condition, you can learn what it means to you. You can take back control of your life and go beyond the limitations of the physical body.

Perhaps you have a life assignment and this illness is essential in learning the lesson you chose to master. This does not mean that you should give up, but continue to examine your pain and learn to accept your highest good. The healing power of the Universe flows through you at your request. Feel this energy flow through you!

You cannot force your body to heal, you allow it to heal. Accept your body just as it is; love it with its pain and illness. Surround your condition with compassion and love. Love and joy are the greatest healers of all. Love your body with its perfection and its imperfection. Love and accept your illness; it is a tool from which you can benefit. Look inside yourself and ask your higher Self what message this illness brings you. What can this illness teach you? How can it help you grow? What good can you find in experiencing it? Learn its lesson and let it go.

Affirm that you are free of negativity and pain. Forgive all who have hurt you. Forgive yourself. Replace destructive feelings with soothing, healing Light and let vitality and energy come into your body. You are divinely protected and you are never alone. Your Divine Plan is unfolding as it should.

Quiet Reflection

Sit or lie down with your spine straight. Yawn and s t r e t c h. Close your eyes. Breathe deeply, relax, and let all your muscles go limp. Feel a stream of Light-filled Energy beaming down from the cosmos and flowing up from the earth. Let this Light flow harmoniously through your body, mind, and spirit, and radiate from every part of your being. Keep breathing deeply and slowly while you go to a quiet place inside yourself. Count back from 10 to 1, relaxing more with each deep breath. Visualize the following:

Walk up the path once more to the crystal palace you have created in your heart. Go to the waterfall and stream that have healed you and given you strength. Imagine a pool of warm, clear water that is protected from the rushing current of the waterfall. This water is pure health and peace. Test this calm water with your toes—it feels so inviting! Slowly let your whole body slip into the water. Feel it soothe you, taking away worry and tight muscles. Let yourself go completely limp and relax totally. Allow waves of relaxation to flow through you. Breathe in divine love and Light. As you inhale, see the air you breathe as pure, white Light. This healing light surrounds any pain, sickness, or negativity that you might have. Hold the Light around your pain. As you exhale, allow the pain, sickness, or negativity to exit with your breath. Picture it leaving your body and dissolving into nothingness. Continue to inhale healing Light and exhale sadness and pain as long as you wish. Relax. Enjoy the soothing water; the Light; the love. Say to yourself, "The strength of the Universe surrounds me and makes me strong. Peace fills me and makes me calm. Love flows through me and fills me with joy. I love and accept my body. What I can change, I will change with strength; that which I cannot change, I accept lovingly as a perfect part of who I am. I am strong in body, mind, and spirit. I grow

stronger each new moment. The past is gone; I let it go. My life is unfolding in Divine right order. My highest good is unfolding with each new day. I give thanks to a higher Source for this perfect Universe and for the perfect plan of my life. My body's healing power joins the power of the Universe and confusion and sickness are washed away. Only powerful, loving energy remains."

Imagine healing energy flowing through your body, clearing away all impurities and sicknesses and dissolving them into nothingness. This healing energy continues to flow through your body. You are filled with strength; every cell in your body is healthy and perfect. You are totally relaxed. All stress and pain have melted away into nothingness.

When you choose to leave, peace, balance, and good health go with you. Healing energy will continue to flow through you, keeping you strong and feeling your best.

Enjoy this feeling of peace for as long as you wish. When you are ready, take a deep breath and begin to move your hands and feet. Stretch and open your eyes.

Family's Request for the Ill

Relax. Get comfortable. Ask that the healing energy of the Higher Power of the Universe fill you and flow through you.

This is a request for healing energy to fill (name) and lift his/her pain for his/her highest good. The energy we send is not our own; it will not deplete us. It will fill us with the same healing energy that we request be sent to (name). Two of us together requesting Light-filled energy are more powerful than two of us apart. We ask that even if we are not physically together, that our requests be joined and that our power be intensified in our unity. We ask that the highest good occur, with no force or interference. Our intent is to send (name) healing energy. This energy is to go wherever (name)'s highest Self wishes to direct it. We wish to help (name) understand his/her pain and in doing so lift it, for his/her highest good and greatest joy. We send this healing energy to (name) in love.

Visualize (name) lying comfortably, with his/her spine straight and arms at his/her sides. His/her legs are uncrossed and in a straight line with his/her body. Imagine all of us standing in a circle around (name)'s bed. Healing angels are standing in a circle behind us, protecting all of us and drawing healing power to us as well. See Light fill the room. All is perfect; all is peaceful. We lift up our arms toward the sky, and we are light as air. Healing light flows down into the room; it is a powerful force, yet gentle and loving. See this energy enter (name) through the top of his/her head. As it enters, (name) is filled with amazing peace and warmth. All is well. This energy flows down (name)'s spine; he/she can feel the tingle of healing energy flowing through him/her. This energy radiates from his/her spine and flows along the nerve passages into every part of his/her body, mind, and spirit. Down his/her arms and legs this healing,

loving energy flows, radiating from his/her body, filling him/her with peace and perfect health. All that (name) needs to know is revealed to him/her. With this highest understanding comes release. All negativity, fear, and pain are lifted from (name)'s body, mind, and spirit and are dissolved into nothingness. Healing energy continues to flow from the Highest Source and into (name)'s body. All pain is lifted; only healing, loving energy remains. Whatever is for (name)'s highest good comes to him/her now. This peaceful, loving energy will remain with (name) and with us. (Name) will move with ease and burdens that he/she didn't even know existed will be lifted. Everything happens for (name)'s highest good with no force or interference to his/her highest plan. This request for healing is a testament of our love for (name) and the love that exists for us. We ask that this energy we have shared also bring each and every one of us our highest good. So be it. So it is.

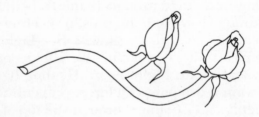

Message From Within

Your connection with your higher Self becomes stronger each time you listen to your inner knowing. Write questions about what you desire to understand about your health. Relax; be open and the truth will come. Write down any messages you receive.

Take Action

What will you do to help you become more healthy in each of
the following areas of your life?

Eating/Drinking

Exercise

Breathing

Emotions

Recreation

Relationships

Rest/Relaxation

Spirituality

Work/School

What is your biggest health concern?

Describe actions you can take to become more healthy.

Burning Desire

I have a burning desire to heal myself
with pure, loving energy.

Affirmations

I lovingly take care of my emotions
and my body.
I learn to understand strong feelings,
then I let them flow away from me
and dissolve into nothingness.
I inhale healing Light.
I exhale all negativity.
I forgive all who have brought me pain;
I release the past.
The healing power of the Universe
flows through me and makes me strong.

My Personal Affirmations

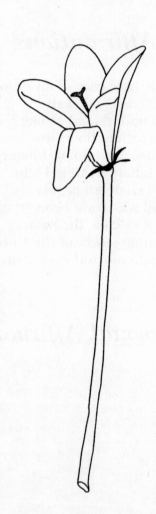

20

Work Through Your Grief

E.J. Rogers

When you are sorrowful look again in your heart, and you shall see that in truth you are weeping for that which has been your delight.

—Kahlil Gibran

Work Through Your Grief

One of the hardest experiences you ever face is the illness or death of a loved one. Since what lies beyond death is unknown to most, it is feared. Society does not prepare you. Death is not usually discussed, and you do not examine your feelings and beliefs about it until it comes into your life. It is difficult to deal with your grief and at the same time search for comfort and an understanding of death.

Examine your feelings about death and life after death now when you can think clearly. Don't wait until you are faced with it. Discover the truth of how you feel deep inside you. Renew your beliefs about the Higher Power of the Universe; a strong belief system will give you much consolation at times of extreme grief or loss. Strengthen your ability to draw upon this loving Energy of which you are a part.

The death of the physical body happens to every living being. It is a vital part of earthly existence. Death sets time limits, giving an urgency to "do it now" before it is too late. The body serves you well in this life; it has an end when it is no longer needed. Death is one more step on a miraculous journey that does not cease when life on earth is completed.

When the higher Self has completed what it has come to accomplish it finds a way out of its earthly existence. A fatal accident or illness can be that way for the spirit to leave the body. Even though you do not see it or always know what it is, there is a Divine Plan for each living being; an order and a plan for every occurrence. As surely as there is a Plan that lets the earth circle the sun, that allows spring to follow winter, that lets the heart beat without conscious help, there is order and purpose in your existence.

Death is not a punishment and is no one's "fault." It is not meant to keep you in despair. Take each small hurt and deal with it in a loving and constructive manner. When the emotional pain of illness and death comes, as it does for everyone, you will be better able to cope.

Look to nature for an understanding of the Divine Plan for life and death. Death is as natural as the sun setting at dusk. You see the sun come up each morning, and so it is with you. As the sun goes down, it is also rising; out of sight, but rising again all the same.

Your very existence shows you miracle after miracle. You cannot see the air you breathe and yet it keeps you alive. You do not see electricity and yet you believe that it is real and that it will perform. You cannot see the individual atoms that make up your body and yet science tells you that you are energy in motion.

On earth, you experience beginnings and endings. With the death of a loved one you might see this passing as a final goodbye—it is not! The spirit lives forever. Human understanding is limited, but you do not need proof to know the validity of your deepest knowing—trust the truth your heart whispers to you.

You now exist. With that majestic fact alone, it is not hard to imagine that you can exist forever. Discover your beliefs within the wisdom of your own heart.

Those who have died are now cradled in the loving arms of the Universe. Even with this belief you will have immense grief because of the physical separation. Death is a vital part of each human being's Divine Plan. It is not a conscious decision, but a decision of the higher Self. Their jobs are completed; their lessons learned or taught. They did not desert you, although feeling that they did is a reaction you might have for a time. Whatever your feelings are, they are okay.

There is no "right" or "wrong" way to feel. But you must deal with your grief. Ignoring your pain does not make it go away, it makes it get worse. Face your feelings. Read about death; talk to someone; become involved with a group. Let your feelings out.

Emotions will overwhelm you and sometimes the pain may seem unbearable. Time does not heal all pain, but over time you learn to deal with your grief. Breathe deeply. Let your emotions surface. Cry; with tears comes release.

Everything you experience helps you fulfill your Divine Plan. You can take what life brings you and grow from it, or you can see only negativity and let it destroy your life. In this life you are here to learn and grow in love and wisdom. Your greatest teacher is pain.

Examine each incident life brings you and search for the good in it; find something of value in every experience. Make a positive change in your life because of what you learn.

Examine your pain. Would you give up the pain of loss and separation if that also meant giving up the time you spent with your loved one? It is proof of the love and joy you once shared.

Time will allow you to discover your new existence with your loved one—you are physically apart, but always together in your heart. Your loved one is only a thought away. You can communicate now in your mind's eye. Surround your loved one with Light-filled Energy, and open your heart and let his or her love heal your pain. Your loved one will always be with you in spirit.

Your loved one is perfectly safe, free from pain, filled with peace and full awareness of his or her higher Self. Magnificent love surrounds and fills him or her with delight.

By your gradual acceptance, you will help your loved one continue to grow in love on the other side. Soothe his or her heart as you soothe your own. Release and comfort him or her by showing that you understand the hard lessons this has taught you. Your loved one has brought you a magnificent gift. Deep in your innermost knowing lie secrets of what his or her being with you meant. Search for the reasons of your loved one's life, not for the reasons of his or her death.

Life on this earth is short and precious. This moment is what we will always have and on which we can always depend.

Life is a gift from a higher Power, and death is a part of life that need not be feared. It is a passing over into new and eternal life. Unlike our earthly existence, there was no beginning and there will be no end in eternity. Continue to grow in love until you become one with unlimited Power and Light.

Learn to connect with the Energy that awaits you. Let the Light and Love of the Universe flow through you and bring you peace, and ask for strength and understanding to fill you and help you through your most difficult times. You are discovering the perfection of who you really are. Turn to the Light and discover the peace and love that wait for you!

Quiet Reflection

Sit or lie down with your spine straight. Yawn and s t r e t c h. Close your eyes. Breathe deeply, relax, and let all your muscles go limp. Feel a stream of Light-filled Energy beaming down from the cosmos and flowing up from the earth. Let this Light flow harmoniously through your body, mind, and spirit, and radiate from every part of your being. Keep breathing deeply and slowly while you go to a quiet place inside yourself. Count back from 10 to 1, relaxing more with each deep breath. Visualize the following:

You are sitting on velvety grass and leaning against a sturdy tree near your Light-filled crystal palace. A balmy breeze is blowing; the sun is warm upon your face. A magnificent white bird with powerful wings comes to you. You perch safely on the bird's feathered back and up, up you soar toward the powerful energy of the sun. The sun's heat becomes your heat; its energy becomes your energy. You are one with the sun. The energy of the Universe flows through you—feel the power! Experience your unity and love with All That Is. Send your love to everything and everyone who ever existed. All is as it should be. Feel the joy that belongs to you. All negativity and sadness are transformed into positive energy, and only truth, power, and light remain. Enjoy the reality of your power and loving energy. With each breath you become more peaceful, loving, and strong. Anything you need to know is revealed to you.

When you are ready, come back to the earth on the wings of the bird. Lean once more against the strong, sturdy tree. Sink down on the soft grass. Feel the solid earth beneath you give you peace.

Enjoy this feeling of peace for as long as you wish. When you are ready, take a deep breath and begin to move your hands and feet. Stretch and open your eyes.

Message From Within

What are your beliefs regarding a Higher Power? How do you feel about life after death and eternity? Become still and write down anything at all that comes to mind.

Take Action

What are your beliefs concerning a Higher Power?

What do you feel happens to a person's spirit after death?

What would help you most if a loved one became seriously ill or died?

Why do you think you came to this earth?

Angel Wings

With tousled hair and eyes so huge,
And a voice as soft as air;
A heart as big as life itself,
I look but don't see her there.

Far better to feel the pain of goodbye
Than never to have loved her at all.
Look to the reasons for her life,
Not why the angels called.

As a caterpillar, so are we,
We change but do not die;
We break our shell and fly free,
As does the butterfly.

Some see death as an end,
Rather it is a glorious start.
Illusions abound on this earth,
They confuse the human heart.

The sun sets before your eyes,
It's gone, it's out of sight;
Yet it is rising on the other side,
Warming all and giving light.

Always near but not here to see;
Together in our dreams.
We'll meet one day in eternity,
And soar on angel wings.

—Elizabeth J. Rogers
August 1991

Burning Desire

I have a burning desire to discover
the truth of eternity
deep within myself.

Affirmations

I am one with the Divine Whole.
Love, energy, and wisdom
surge through me
and burst forth triumphantly!
I am blossoming like an
eternal flower.
My Divine Plan is unfolding
exactly as it should.
My inner wisdom pours forth all the
information and knowledge I need.
The Light is with me;
I am the Light.

My Personal Affirmations

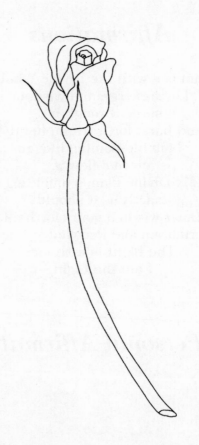

21

Live In This Moment

Be intent upon the perfection of the present day.

—William Law

Live In This Moment

This moment is the only moment you can direct. Yesterday is gone; tomorrow is always in the future. Don't allow people or events from the past to destroy your enjoyment of this moment. Don't delay being happy and satisfied until "later." Create peace in each moment and you will create lasting joy.

Nothing is enough until you are enough, as you are right now. You will not be happy with what you achieve or accumulate until you can be happy with what you now have and are. If you wait for someone or something in the future to bring you happiness, it may never come.

The joy of taking constructive actions is one of life's greatest rewards. Positive actions put you in control of your life. When you are in control, you feel good about yourself and that your life is worthwhile.

Define your purpose in life. Develop a clear idea of who you are at your best and what you want to accomplish. Write down goals and a plan of action to achieve what you desire.

Enjoy goals while you are achieving them. Create happiness now by taking actions you find constructive and beneficial. Take charge of what you think and what you do in the present moment. Make positive changes and decide what is the most important action to take. Focus on what you are doing now until it is accomplished.

You have everything you need to be happy at this very moment. Happiness comes from inside yourself, not from possessions and other people. Create joy with the way you and your life are right now.

Quiet Reflection

Sit or lie down with your spine straight. Yawn and s t r e t c h. Close your eyes. Breathe deeply, relax, and let all your muscles go limp. Feel a stream of Light-filled Energy beaming down from the cosmos and flowing up from the earth. Let this Light flow harmoniously through your body, mind, and spirit, and radiate from every part of your being. Keep breathing deeply and slowly while you go to a quiet place inside yourself. Count back from 10 to 1, relaxing more with each deep breath. Visualize the following:

Imagine it is daybreak. Today is a new day; a new beginning. You are enjoying the cozy warmth of a bed of clean, soft leaves deep within a lush, protected forest near your crystal palace. Feel yourself grow roots and send them deep into the rich, nourishing soil. Become one with the earth. Your roots go deeper and deeper into the life-giving earth. Experience the earth's strength and peace. The sun rises; its light fills you with invigorating warmth and energy. Reach out and take the sunlight into your arms. Feel the energy of the Universe flow through you and feel yourself grow larger and larger. Your spirit embraces the forest, your state, and the whole country. You expand until you are one with the planet. Your spirit continues to grow until you become one with the Universe; one with all of creation. Radiate your love and energy to the world around you. No matter what the weather, the energy of the sun and the strength of the earth will remain with you.

Enjoy this feeling of peace for as long as you wish. When you are ready, take a deep breath and begin to move your hands and feet. Stretch and open your eyes.

Message From Within

Discover your life's perfect plan. What is your natural ability? What makes you feel joyous, fulfilled, and alive? Let your own wisdom and creativity pour forth. Let the truth of who you are be revealed to you. Write down all the thoughts and feelings that emerge from the deepest part of your being.

Take Action

What is your purpose in life? What do you enjoy doing most of all? What do you do well?

Describe the person you want to be.

Describe the life you want to live.

Each morning, make a list of things that you will accomplish that day. Do the most important thing on your list first. Then go to the second most important thing on your list and continue until your list has been completed.

Burning Desire

I have a burning desire
to live fully in this moment.

Affirmations

This day is the most important day;
this moment
is the most important moment!
I give this moment my full attention.
I cherish each moment
for the precious gift it is.
I give thanks for the happiness
I feel right now.
Surprise follows
blissful surprise.

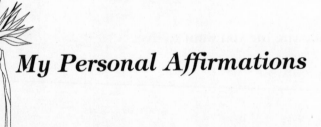

My Personal Affirmations

22

Look to the Future with Joy

... if you do follow your bliss you put yourself on a kind of track that has been there all the while, waiting for you, and the life that you ought to be living is the one you are living. When you can see that, you begin to meet people who are in the field of your bliss, and they open the doors to you. I say, follow your bliss and don't be afraid, and doors will open where you didn't know they were going to be.

—Joseph Campbell

Look to the Future with Joy

The Universe holds unlimited abundance for you—enjoy its beauty and generosity. Thinking constructive thoughts will pave the way to taking positive actions. Pursue your highest plan and allow doors to swing open before you. Actively following your heart's desire will create joy in your present as well as your future.

If there is something you can do now for your future, do it! Don't waste energy worrying about tomorrow. Plan your future and put all your energy into fulfilling your plan. Set goals so the dreams you hold in your heart become a reality. Take action! Don't wait—do it now!

It is easy to take positive action if you focus your thoughts on the successful completion of your goals. Your thoughts have powerful energy. Visualize clearly what you want in your life. Picture it vividly, as if it has already occurred. What you think your future will be, you will create!

Enjoy the present while working toward a goal. Do not put off your happiness until a particular goal is achieved or you have acquired a certain possession, but enjoy the process. This will create joy now as well as in your future. Your feelings of joy and vitality let you know you are going where you truly want to go.

Working toward goals that are for your highest good raises your self-image. These goals help you respect yourself, inspire you to be the best you can be, and encourage you to take action. Positive action now will also give you the belief in a safe and abundant future.

You are on this earth to learn and grow. What is appropriate for you today may change tomorrow as it has changed from yesterday. Continue to reevaluate your beliefs and your goals to help you take the most important action for the present and the future.

When a goal is updated or accomplished, continue to move forward. Set goals on an ongoing basis so you can clearly see the most significant action to take. You will know where you are going and what your future holds. Your actions will be what you have decided upon. You, and only you, direct your own life. Have goals and go forward on the path of your highest good.

The creativity of the Universe is a part of you. Let it flourish inside you and pour forth from you. Find fulfillment in each moment and look to the future with joy!

Quiet Reflection

Sit or lie down with your spine straight. Yawn and s t r e t c h. Close your eyes. Breathe deeply, relax, and let all your muscles go limp. Feel a stream of Light-filled Energy beaming down from the cosmos and flowing up from the earth. Let this Light flow harmoniously through your body, mind, and spirit, and radiate from every part of your being. Keep breathing deeply and slowly while you go to a quiet place inside yourself. Count back from 10 to 1, relaxing more with each deep breath. Visualize the following:

The special crystal palace you have created in your mind's eye always waits for you. Here you can experience the highest part of your creative Self. Everything you imagine you can create. Come here often to dream; to play; to create. Imagine a goal you have chosen to accomplish: picture exactly what you want to happen as if it is taking place right now. Feel yourself taking action. Focus only on your good and feel the joy of taking action. Feel the satisfaction of directing your own life—doing what you have chosen to do; doing what you love to do. Imagine you already have what you want. Experience it being in your life right now! Think the thoughts and feel the emotions that you will experience when your goal is fulfilled. Imagine white Light flowing down from the Universal Source. Your loving energy joins with the energy of the Universe and gives life to your dream. Feel joyous and full of life! Everything you desire already belongs to you. Your highest good is now creating and attracting what it needs to be fulfilled.

Enjoy this feeling of peace for as long as you wish. When you are ready, take a deep breath and begin to move your hands and feet. Stretch and open your eyes.

Message From Within

Messages from your higher Self come to you through your thoughts, feelings, and images. What is the most important goal you want to accomplish in this lifetime? Let the knowledge of all you need to understand flow to you. Write down anything that comes to you.

Take Action

Put your goals in writing or they are nothing more than feeble wishes. Decide on a goal that you firmly believe you can achieve and that you are committed to accomplishing. Write down this goal in detail, then outline briefly what needs to be done.

Be creative and write down a plan of action. Note the steps you might take. Let your inner wisdom flow! Jot down any ideas that come, no matter how outrageous or seemingly impossible.

Jot down what problems/challenges you might encounter when you take action to fulfill your goal.

Be wildly creative once more about how you might overcome these challenges.

Choose the best steps to take. Make a note of the order in which they will be taken and the date by which each step will be completed. Now rewrite your plan in detail.

Jot down how you will benefit from achieving this goal. Note the positive feelings that you will experience as a result of working toward and accomplishing this goal.

Write your goal as an affirmation—let it read as though your goal is now accomplished.

Read your affirmation and experience it! Feel the emotions of success. Enjoy the benefits and positive feelings you described above. Picture your "accomplished" goal often; give it life in your imagination. Carry this affirmation with you and experience it often.

Take action! Take the first step you decided upon and complete it. Then take the second step, and the third ... Remember to enjoy achieving your goal! Occasionally review your plan of action and make adjustments as necessary. Never give up! You haven't failed until you stop trying. You can do whatever you desire to do.

When you are nearing the completion of your goal, set another. Continue this process throughout your life and you will always know where you are going and what action to take.

Burning Desire

I have a burning desire to look to
the future with joy.

Affirmations

I am a child of the Universe,
a creation of inner wisdom and love.
I am divinely protected and guided.
My higher Self reveals to me
my life's perfect plan.
The joy and abundance of
the loving Universe flow to me.
What is mine by divine right comes to me
for my greatest joy and my highest good.
The love and wisdom of the Universe
flow through me forever and ever.

My Personal Affirmations

23

Share Your Love

A human being is part of the whole, called by us "Universe," a part limited in time and space. He experiences himself, his thoughts and feelings, as something separated from the rest—a kind of optical delusion of his consciousness. This delusion is a kind of prison for us, restricting us to our personal desires and to affection for a few persons nearest to us. Our task must be to free ourselves from this prison by widening our circle of compassion to embrace all living creatures and the whole of nature in its beauty.

—Albert Einstein

Share Your Love

Even as separate beings we are united as one—love is the thread that connects us all. When you think or act with love you are in harmony with the Universe and you feel you are moving in a positive, upward direction. When you act without love your disharmony shows you that you are lost. Listen to your innermost guidance—it lights the way to truth and happiness.

Love brings joy, better health, and vitality. It inspires you and gives your life meaning. Share yourself and develop closeness with the people in your life. Make eye contact and occasionally be the first to say hello. Smile—it is the language of acceptance everyone understands. Love is your true path. Love and be joyous and full of life!

Love and accept the inner beauty of yourself and others, unconditionally and unselfishly. Love is not given with expectation of reward, guilt, or fear of loss; love is given with joy. Love for the pure delight of it!

Listen to what others say and try to understand how they feel. Let your true feelings be known in a calm, reasonable way. Do not judge others or their actions, but let them proceed at their own pace. Negativity keeps you from love, and love will guard and protect you from negativity. Turn on your power and let understanding and kindness flow.

You have an obligation to all of creation to put light and love into the Universe. Love yourself fully! Let the well-being of others be as important as your own. Bring harm to no one you meet; treat others as you wish to be treated. Care about others and help them help themselves. Encourage and assist others but trust them enough to find their own perfect way. For the deepest satisfaction, do something that gives love back to the Universe. When you give unselfishly of yourself, love and energy flow to you in abundance.

Your smile and loving thoughts surround yourself and others with positive energy. Send this energy that bubbles in you to the Universe around you. Love is with you and radiates from you; love is what you are. Share your smile and your love with the world!

Quiet Reflection

Sit or lie down with your spine straight. Yawn and s t r e t c h. Close your eyes. Breathe deeply, relax, and let all your muscles go limp. Feel a stream of Light-filled Energy beaming down from the cosmos and flowing up from the earth. Let this Light flow harmoniously through your body, mind, and spirit, and radiate from every part of your being. Keep breathing deeply and slowly while you go to a quiet place inside yourself. Count back from 10 to 1, relaxing more with each deep breath. Visualize the following:

Imagine a golden egg-shaped Light-form before you. This golden Light is pure protection and complete love. Put all the positive feelings you wish to experience inside this form. It grows to be larger than your physical body. Fill this golden egg-shaped form with all the love you ever needed and wanted. Now step into this golden Light and experience all the love it holds for you.

When you are ready, picture a person with whom you wish to share your love. Visualize this person as peaceful and loving. Imagine the golden Light-filled egg growing larger still, surrounding this person and nourishing and comforting him or her.

Think to yourself, "You and I are united by love. I respect the wisdom and the beauty inside you. I accept you exactly as you are. I send you positive, loving energy. Use this energy for your greatest joy, your highest good, and for the highest good of all." Imagine this thought-energy intensifying the golden Light that surrounds you both. The love and energy of the Universe flows through you, and you are one with all creation. Go forward in love, harmony, and peace.

Enjoy this feeling of peace for as long as you wish. When you are ready, take a deep breath and begin to move your hands and feet. Stretch and open your eyes.

Message From Within

Contact with your higher Self becomes natural with true desire and by opening yourself to this communication often. Trust your highest knowing to reveal what you need to understand about sharing your love. Write down any messages that come to you.

Take Action

How do you (or how will you) show yourself unconditional love?

How do you (or how will you) show unconditional love and acceptance to your family?

How do you show respect to the people you encounter?

Do you smile and make eye contact when you pass or first meet a person? Begin to do this! Note how this positive flow of energy lets you feel.

What can you do to share your love and make this Universe a better place to live for all of us?

Join your love with the energy of the Universe. Create joy— what you think is what you get!

Burning Desire

I have a burning desire to share
my love with the world.

Affirmations

We all are created and loved
by the same Power.
I surround others with loving energy
to use for their highest good
and their greatest joy.
I rejoice at the love
that pours to me and from me.
I love, and I am joyous and alive!
The Universe fills me with
harmony and love.
Love is what I am.

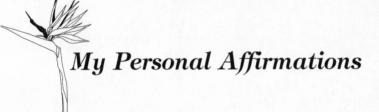

My Personal Affirmations

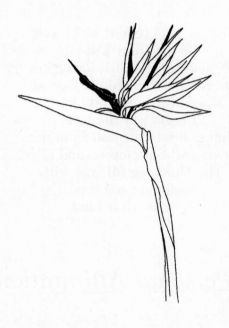

24

Create Joy!

... a man, who as a physical being is always turned toward the outside, thinking that his happiness lies outside him, finally turns inward and discovers that the source is within him.

—Soren Kierkegaard

Create Joy!

You have everything you need to be happy right now. Joy comes from inside you; it is determined by your thoughts and nothing else—not cars, clothes, homes, power, or other people. These things may bring you pleasure for a short time, but those pleasures do not last.

Create joy by being your best, not by acquiring objects. You must be happy within yourself before you will be able to enjoy possessions. Learn to love and accept yourself in the present and you will learn to create happiness now. Unless happiness bubbles through you as you are and with what you have at the present, you may not find it.

Let go of past pain. Experience and work through grief that may linger with you. Forgive all who have hurt you, and forgive yourself. Let go of past teachings and beliefs and live the best life for you. Be free of old habits and thought patterns and make new choices. Take action and fulfill your dreams.

Go within and find the truth of who you really are. Breathe deeply, relax, and take time to discover your inner Self. Join with the Power of the Universe. Experience yourself in your highest glory and let yourself be that beautiful, genuine being.

Discover your life's perfect plan—what is your life's purpose? What do you love to do? Develop and use your talents.

Be optimistic and full of delight. Act toward achieving your highest good. Set goals and visualize your life as you desire it to be. What you experience in your mind draws energy to make it a reality. Do the most important activity first. This may sometimes be work, but not always; relaxation and play are vital, too. Whatever you choose to be the most essential action to take, do it joyfully!

If you want to be joyous, do what brings happiness to you. Listen to inspiring music or a motivational tape. Meditate on the beauty and perfection of the Universe. Read an uplifting book; take a quick shower; talk to someone who is optimistic and full of energy. Spend time with a favorite hobby. Do something for someone else and bring happiness to you both. Sing at the top of your voice. Enjoy the beauty of nature. Take a walk, run, or dance. Give someone—or your-self—a hug. Smile and your spirits will soar. Entice yourself to laugh! Delight in the good which is now yours and appreciate the perfection of your highest Self. Take a moment and give thanks for the abundance and the wonder in your life. Be glad to be alive!

The Universe is abundant; there will always be enough for everyone. The world is evolving and growing stronger in love. Your positive, loving thoughts and actions make the world a better place.

You are responsible for your thoughts and feelings. Only you can make this moment happy; you direct the way you think and feel. Create joy by thinking joyous thoughts. No one or no thing can give you joy. It is a gift you create in the innermost part of yourself; it waits lovingly for you. Discover the power inside you.

The love, the Light, and the power are with you. Love is what you are. Love and create joy! Think joyous thoughts—what you think is what you create!

Quiet Reflection

Sit or lie down with your spine straight. Yawn and s t r e t c h. Close your eyes. Breathe deeply, relax, and let all your muscles go limp. Feel a stream of Light-filled Energy beaming down from the cosmos and flowing up from the earth. Let this Light flow harmoniously through your body, mind, and spirit, and radiate from every part of your being. Keep breathing deeply and slowly while you go to a quiet place inside yourself. Count back from 10 to 1, relaxing more with each deep breath. Visualize the following:

Race up the path to your sparkling crystal palace. Experience the happiness that is all around you; reach out and bring it into your heart. Become one with nature. Hug a tree and become one with it! Grow roots and send them deep into the rich soil and feed on the nourishment of the earth. Just be. Feel the sunshine's warmth give you life. Spread your limbs and contribute to the beauty and energy of the Universe. Now reach to the sky. What a glorious blue! Float on the fluffy clouds. Become a raindrop; follow its path from the cloud to the earth to the stream, down a waterfall to the river to the sea. Become one with every animal on the earth. Swim; crawl; stand; walk on all fours; fly! Feel the breeze blow through your hair. Smell the fresh, sweet air. Gently touch the earth; feel the solid ground beneath your feet. Everything is just as it should be. Listen to the music that is everywhere around you—hear birds chirping, a baby cooing, the child inside you laughing. You are one with all creation. Be comforted by the beauty, wonder, and perfection of this magnificent Universe. Be happy!

Enjoy this feeling of peace for as long as you wish. When you are ready, take a deep breath and begin to move your hands and feet. Stretch and open your eyes.

Message From Within

Relax. Free your mind of logical thought. Be open to pure ideas of a joyous nature; open your heart to energy and inspiration. Write down all that comes to you from the truest part of your being.

Take Action

List the activities you enjoy. What feelings do these activities bring you?

List the people you enjoy being with. What feelings do you have when you are with these people?

Make a list of the places you enjoy being; note why you enjoy being there. What feelings do you have when you are in these places?

Describe the way you feel when you create joy in your life. Note what brings you these feelings.

Be happy! Now is the time to create joy in your life!

Burning Desire

I have a burning desire
to create a full and joyous life.

Affirmations

I am thankful for what I have.
Success and abundance fill my life.
I open to the perfection of who I am.
I love myself deeply and fully.
Happiness is a gift
I generously give myself.
I look forward in awe
to the pleasures that await me.

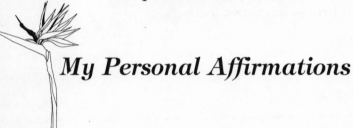

My Personal Affirmations

Works Which Have Influenced My Writing

Bach, Richard. *Bridge Across Forever.* Dell Publishing Co., Inc., 1986.

Bartholomew. *I Come As A Brother: A Remembrance of Illusions.* High Mesa Press, 1988.

Buscaglia, Leo. *Loving Each Other.* SLACK, Inc., 1984.

Crum, Jessie K. *The Art of Inner Listening.* The Theosophical Publishing House, 1984.

Dowling, Collette. *The Cinderella Complex.* Pocket Books, 1982.

Gawain, Shakti. *Creative Visualization.* Whatever Publishing, Inc., 1982.

Gawain, Shakti. *Living in the Light.* New World Library, 1986.

Gibran, Kahlil. *The Prophet.* Alfred A. Knopf, 1973.

Hay, Louise L. *Morning and Evening Meditations.* Cassette tape. Hay House.

Hay, Louise L. *Self Healing: Creating Your Own Health.* Cassette tape. Hay House.

Hill, Napoleon. *Think and Grow Rich.* Fawcett Crest, 1963.

Hittleman, Richard. *Yoga U.S.A.* Bantam, 1968.

Hopkins, Tom. *The Official Guide to Success.* Champion Press, 1982.

James, Muriel and Dorothy Jongeward. *Born To Win.* Addison-Wesley Publishing Company, Inc., 1971.

Keyes, Jr., Ken. *Handbook to Higher Consciousness.* Love Line Books, 1988.

Lecron, Leslie M. *Self Hypnotism: The Technique And Its Use In Daily Living.* Prentice-Hall, Inc., 1970.

Murphy, Dr. Joseph. *The Power of Your Subconscious Mind.* Prentice-Hall, Inc., 1988.

Norvell, Anthony. *Metaphysics: New Dimensions of the Mind.* Parker Publishing Company, Inc., 1977.

Peale, Dr. Norman Vincent. *The Power of Positive Thinking.* Prentice-Hall, 1954.

Rodegast, Pat and Judith Stanton. *Emmanuel's Book.* Bantam, 1987.

Shinn, Florence Scovel. *The Game of Life and How to Play It, The Power of the Spoken Word, Your Word is Your Wand,* and *The Secret Door to Success.* A four-book set. DeVorss & Company, 1978.

Tice, Louis. *Investment in Excellence Seminar.* The Pacific Institute, Inc., Seattle, Washington, 1983.

Two Disciples. *The Rainbow Bridge.* Rainbow Bridge Productions, 1982.

Tracey, Brian. *The Psychology of Achievement.* Cassette tape series.

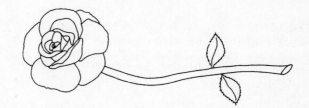

STAY IN TOUCH

On the following pages you will find listed, with their current prices, some of the books now available on related subjects. Your book dealer stocks most of these and will stock new titles in the Llewellyn series as they become available. We urge your patronage.

To obtain our full catalog, to keep informed about new titles as they are released and to benefit from informative articles and helpful news, you are invited to write for our bi-monthly news magazine/catalog, *Llewellyn's New Worlds of Mind and Spirit*. A sample copy is free, and it will continue coming to you at no cost as long as you are an active mail customer. Or you may subscribe for just $10.00 in U.S.A. and Canada ($20.00 overseas, first class mail). Many bookstores also have New Worlds available to their customers. Ask for it.

Stay in touch! In *New Worlds'* pages you will find news and features about new books, tapes and services, announcements of meetings and seminars, articles helpful to our readers, news of authors, products and services, special money-making opportunities, and much more.

Llewellyn's New Worlds of Mind and Spirit
P.O. Box 64383-K354, St. Paul, MN 55164-0383, U.S.A.

* * *

TO ORDER BOOKS AND TAPES

If your book dealer does not have the books described on the following pages readily available, you may order them direct from the publisher by sending full price in U.S. funds, plus $3.00 for postage and handling for orders under $10.00; $4.00 for orders over $10.00. There are no postage and handling charges for orders over $50.00. Postage and handling rates are subject to change. UPS Delivery: We ship UPS whenever possible. Delivery guaranteed. Provide your street address as UPS does not deliver to P.O. Boxes. UPS to Canada requires a $50.00 minimum order. Allow 4-6 weeks for delivery. Orders outside the U.S.A. and Canada: Airmail—add retail price of book; add $5.00 for each non-book item (tapes, etc.); add $1.00 per item for surface mail.

FOR GROUP STUDY AND PURCHASE

Because there is a great deal of interest in group discussion and study of the subject matter of this book, we feel that we should encourage the adoption and use of this particular book by such groups by offering a special quantity price to group leaders or agents.

Our special quantity price for a minimum order of five copies of *Create Your Own Joy* is $30.00 cash-with-order. This price includes postage and handling within the United States. Minnesota residents must add 6.5% sales tax. For additional quantities, please order in multiples of five. For Canadian and foreign orders, add postage and handling charges as above. Credit card (VISA, MasterCard, American Express) orders are accepted. Charge card orders only ($15.00 minimum order) may be phoned in free within the U.S.A. or Canada by dialing 1-800-THE-MOON. For customer service, call 1-612-291-1970. Mail orders to:

LLEWELLYN PUBLICATIONS
P.O. Box 64383-K354, St. Paul, MN 55164-0383, U.S.A.

THE SECRET OF LETTING GO
by Guy Finley

Whether you need to let go of a painful heartache, a destructive habit, a frightening worry or a nagging discontent, *The Secret of Letting Go* shows you how to call upon your own hidden powers and how they can take you through and beyond any challenge or problem. This book reveals the secret source of a brand-new kind of inner strength. In the light of your new and higher self-understanding, emotional difficulties such as loneliness, fear, anxiety and frustration fade into nothingness as you happily discover they never really existed in the first place.

With a foreword by Desi Arnaz Jr., and introduction by Dr. Jesse Freeland, *The Secret of Letting Go* is a pleasing balance of questions and answers, illustrative examples, truth tales, and stimulating dialogues that allow the reader to share in the exciting discoveries that lead up to lasting self-liberation.

This is a book for the discriminating, intelligent, and sensitive reader who is looking for *real* answers.
0-87542-223-3, 240 pgs.,5¼ x 8, softcover $9.95

WHAT YOUR DREAMS CAN TEACH YOU
by Alex Lukeman

Dreams are honest and do not lie. They have much to teach us, but the lessons are often difficult to understand. Confusion comes not from the dream but from the outer mind's attempt to understand it.

What Your Dreams Can Teach You is a workbook of self-discovery, with a systematic and proven approach to the understanding of dreams. It *does not* contain lists of meanings for dream symbols. Only you, the dreamer, can discover what the images in your dreams mean for you. The book *does* contain step-by-step information which can lead you to success with your dreams, success that will bear fruit in your waking hours. Learn to tap into the aspect of yourself that truly knows how to interpret dreams, the inner energy of understanding called the "Dreamer Within." This aspect of your consciousness will lead you to an accurate understanding of your dreams and even assist you with interpreting dreams of others.
0-87542-475-9, 288 pgs., 6 x 9, softcover $12.95

All prices subject to change without notice.

BRIDGES TO SUCCESS & FULFILLMENT
Techniques to Discover & Release Your Potential
by William W. Hewitt
In the tradition of Dale Carnegie and Norman Vincent Peale, William Hewitt's latest book will make you stop and think seriously about yourself and your life. In his trademark easy-reading style, this former IBM executive and motivational trainer offers something *new* in the line of self-improvement: A blend of traditional and non-traditional techniques for dealing successfully with the changes, choices and stresses of our time.

Whether you are going through a divorce, loss of a job, a mid-life crisis, or simply want to get *more* out of life, *Bridges to Success & Fulfillment* provides the tools to build a happier tomorrow. Explore your life purpose, choices, altered states of consciousness, self hypnosis, meditation, prayer, self-talk, spirituality, astrology, dreams, difficult people, death, stretching your mind, committees, suicide, even good old boy networks. Hewitt's gutsy, humorous and common-sense approach will inspire you to take charge of your life, work with your higher consciousness, and begin to set in motion a future that is successful beyond your wildest dreams!
0-87542-323-X, 192 pgs., 5¼ x 8, illus., photos $7.95

THE COMPLETE HANDBOOK OF NATURAL HEALING
by Marcia Starck
Got an itch that won't go away? Want a massage but don't know the difference between Rolfing, Reichian Therapy and Reflexology? Tired of going to the family doctor for minor illnesses that you know you could treat at home—if you just knew how?

Designed to function as a home reference guide (yet enjoyable and interesting enough to be read straight through), this book addresses all natural healing modalities in use today: dietary regimes, nutritional supplements, cleansing and detoxification, vitamins and minerals, herbology, homeopathic medicine and cell salts, traditional Chinese medicine, Ayurvedic medicine, body work therapies, exercise, mental and spiritual therapies, and more. In addition, a section of 41 specific ailments outlines natural treatments for everything from acne to varicose veins.
0-87542-742-1, 416 pgs., 6 x 9, softcover $12.95

All prices subject to change without notice.

RECLAIMING WOMAN'S VOICE
Becoming Whole
by Lesley Shore, Ph.D.

Many of today's difficulties stem from a fundamental imbalance in the core of our world. We have lost our ties with mother Earth and the feminine in our nature. The feminine is suppressed, oppressed—abused. And while everyone suffers the consequences of society's devaluation of the feminine, this book primarily explores its effects on women.

Women's voice finds expression in psychological and psychosomatic symptoms. Many women are depressed or anxious. They are troubled by low self-esteem and suffer from eating disorders and other addictions. They question their beauty and their bodies.

This book shows women how to discover what their symptoms are telling them about their hidden needs and blocked energies. Once the cause of these symptom are found, women can then move on with their lives, become whole human beings, live in harmony with inner rhythms, and finally feel good about themselves.

0-87542-722-7, 208 pgs., 5¼ x 8, softcover $9.95

THE ART OF SELF TALK
Formula for Success
by William W. Hewitt

Talk to yourself and you can become a dynamo of self-achieving power! That is because the spoken word has the exceptional ability to quickly program your subconscious mind. In this entertaining yet serious guide to self-improvement, professional hypnotist William Hewitt teaches you how to talk out loud in a special way to program your mind for success. He presents 20 specific everyday situations—job interviews, arguments with your spouse, blocked creativity—and gives explicit instructions on how to successfully deal with them through the art of self-talk. He also provides instructions on devising your own successful scenarios for unique situations.

Learn to use the self-talk techniques to get your prayers answered, overcome stage fright, open your creative channels, set priorities, throw constructive "temper tantrums," lose weight, quit smoking, release frustrations, better your relationships, conquer fear, accomplish your goals, and in general, make magic happen consistently in your life.

0-87542-334-5, 192 pgs., 5¼ x 8, softcover $7.95

All prices subject to change without notice.

AN INVITATION TO DREAM
Tap the Resources to Inner Wisdom
by Ana Lora Garrard, illus. by Ana Lora Garrard
Reclaim the vibrant, creative part of yourself that dreams! Dreamwork allows you to open secret doors within yourself that only you can know. Many of us don't remember our dreams or we find them strange, chaotic, and distant from our understanding. *An Invitation to Dream* helps you discover for yourself the deeply personal messages within your dream images. Rather than giving worn-out "dictionary definitions," this book embraces the magic of dreams and honors the integrity of the dreamer.

This is a simple, clear, and inspiring dream book—one that teaches you how to listen to the wisdom offered in your dreams so that you can place yourself on your own path of awakening, renewal, and joy. You will learn how to recall your dreams more clearly, and you will learn innovative exercises for dream exploration that incorporate movement, artwork, writing, meditation, and verbal sharing. It also includes answers to basic questions about dreams, and outlines the story of the author's own dream journey. The author's colorful artwork provides a strong, visual presentation that will speak to the limitless dimension of your own creativity.
0-87542-253-5, 272 pgs., 6 x 9, illus., color plates $12.95

THE SECRET WAY OF WONDER
Insights from the Silence
by Guy Finley
Introduction by Desi Arnaz, Jr.
Discover an inner world of wisdom and make miracles happen! Here is a simple yet deeply effective system of illuminating and eliminating the problems of inner mental and emotional life.

The Secret Way of Wonder is an interactive spiritual workbook, offering guided practice for self-study. It is about Awakening the Power of Wonder in yourself. A series of 60 "Wonders" (meditations on a variety of subjects) will stir you in an indescribable manner. This is a bold and bright new kind of book that gently leads us on a journey of Spiritual Alchemy where the journey itself is the destination ... and the destination is our need to be spiritually whole men and women. Most of all, you will find out through self investigation that we live in a friendly, intelligent and living universe that we can reach into and that can reach us.
0-87542-221-7, 192 pgs., 5¼ x 8, softcover $9.95

All prices subject to change without notice.

MEDITATION & HUMAN GROWTH
A Practical Manual for Higher Consciousness
by Genevieve Lewis Paulson
Meditation has many purposes—healing, past life awareness, balance, mental clarity and relaxation are just a few. *Meditation and Human Growth* is a life-long guidebook that focuses on the practice of meditation as a tool for growth and development, as well as for expanding consciousness into other realms. It includes detailed meditations of both a "practical" and more esoteric nature to serve the needs of the complete person. Specific exercises are provided for different areas of life: health of the physical body; wealth in the physical world; emotional well-being; transmuting excess sexual energy; experiencing oneness with the universe; and alignment with the seasonal, lunar and planetary energies.

Meditation is a way of opening into areas that are beyond our normal thinking patterns. In fact, what we now call "altered states" and "peak experiences" will become the normal consciousness of the future. This book is full of techniques for those who wish to claim those higher vibrations and expanded awareness for their lives today.
0-87542-599-2, 224 pgs., 17 illus., softcover $12.95

PERSONAL ALCHEMY
A Handbook of Healing & Self-Transformation
by Amber Wolfe
Personal Alchemy offers the first bold look at the practical use of "Rays" for healing and self-development. Rays are spontaneous energy emanations emitting a specific quality, property or attribute. The Red Ray, for example, represents the energies of life force, survival and strength. When used in conjunction with active imagery, the alchemical properties of the Red Ray can activate independence or realign destructiveness and frustration. *Personal Alchemy* explains each color Ray and Light in depth, teaching the material and encouraging the active participation of the reader.

What's more, this book goes beyond anything else written on the Rays because it contains an extensive set of alchemical correlations that amplify the Ray's powers. Each Ray correlates with a specific element, harmonic sound, aroma, symbol, person, rune, astrological sign, Tarot card, angel, and stone, so there are numerous ways to experience and learn this system of healing magick.
0-87542-890-8, 592 pgs., 7 x 10, illus., softcover $17.95

All prices subject to change without notice.

THE LLEWELLYN PRACTICAL GUIDE TO CREATIVE VISUALIZATION
For the Fulfillment of Your Desires
by Denning & Phillips
All things you will ever want must have their start in your mind. The average person uses very little of the full creative power that is his, potentially. It's like the power locked in the atom—it's all there, but you have to learn to release it and apply it constructively.

If you can see it ... in your mind's eye ... you will have it! It's true: you can have whatever you want, but there are "laws" to mental creation that must be followed. The power of the mind is not limited to, nor limited by, the material world. *Creative Visualization* enables people to reach beyond, into the invisible world of astral and spiritual forces.

Some people apply this innate power without actually knowing what they are doing, and achieve great success and happiness; most people, however, use this same power, again unknowingly, incorrectly, and experience bad luck, failure, or at best an unfulfilled life.

This book changes that. Through an easy series of step-by-step, progressive exercises, your mind is applied to bring desire into realization! Wealth, power, success, happiness, even psychic powers ... even what we call magickal power and spiritual attainment ... all can be yours. You can easily develop this completely natural power, and correctly apply it, for your immediate and practical benefit. Illustrated with unique, "puts-you-into-the-picture" visualization aids.
0-87542-183-0, 294 pgs., 5¼ x 8, illus., softcover $8.95